Streets Raised Me, *God* Saved Me

Rondell F Kinsey Jr

Streets Raised Me, God Saved Me.

Copyright © 2024 Rondell F Kinsey Jr

All rights reserved.

Streets Raised Me, God Saved Me.

DEDICATION

I dedicate this to my great-grandma, Ms. Elizabeth Kinsey. You have been my backbone, my reason for wanting to change my life. You never gave up on me and forgave me for all the wrong I've done. I owe this to you. Thank you!

To my grandfather, Theodis Kinsey: even though we don't always see eye to eye, I know you always want the best for me. I love and admire you just as you are. To my grandma, Carolyn, may God bless your soul.

To my godparents, Emery and Mary Kinsey: you hold a special place in my heart.

To my sisters, Tanita, Patrecka, and Kyiaya, and my birth mother, Darlene Ragland: I love you all dearly.

To all my nieces and nephews!

And lastly, to my baby brother, Benny: you mean the world to me, little brother, and I want you to know that.

Streets Raised Me, God Saved Me.

TABLE OF CONTENTS

1 THE POWER OF CHOICE *10*

2 LIVE YOUR CHOICE *15*

3 GETTING OUT YOUR OWN WAY *26*

4 TRUTH BE TOLD *40*

5 LET GO AND LET GOD *55*

6 LETTING GO OF THE PAST *67*

7 PUT DOWN YOUR PHONE AND PICK UP YOUR BIBLE *103*

8 PAIN INTO PURPOSE *116*

9 WALK OF FAITH *127*

10 MISERY INTO MINISTRY *145*

11 WHO BUT YOU? *164*

12 A NEW YOU *181*

About the Author 195

ACKNOWLEDGMENTS

First and Foremost

In the echoing chambers of gratitude, my voice reverberates with the deepest praise for the divine orchestrator of life's grand tapestry. To my savior, Yeshua, your boundless sacrifice echoes through the ages, an anthem of redemption that reaches the depths of my soul. Each passing moment, my love for you swells, an ever-blooming blossom in the garden of faith.

A Beacon of Hope

To the stalwart companions of White Deer Run and Helio Health "Elements," you are the guiding stars in my journey through the tempest of addiction. Amidst the storms, your steady hands and unwavering support have charted a course to calmer seas, and for that, I am eternally grateful.

Mentors and Guides

To my shepherd in Christ, Pastor Ike, your wisdom has been the compass guiding me along the path of righteousness. Through your example, I have learned the true meaning of spiritual fortitude and the strength found in humility. To my counselors and confidants, Jill F, Ms. Shameka, and the illustrious Ms. Jeanette, your belief in my potential has been a beacon of hope in my darkest hours.

Angels Among Us

In the heavens above, my guardian angels watch over me with unwavering love and protection. To my mother, aunt, and legal guardian, Ms. Cynthia Kinsey, your earthly presence may have passed, but your spirit remains a guiding light in the depths of my soul. To my legendary father, Rondell "Big Nique" Kinsey, your legacy of love and strength continues to inspire me each day.

In Memoriam

To my niece, Tierra "Tnewt" Newton, your absence is a poignant reminder of life's fleeting nature. Though parted by the veil of mortality, your spirit lives on in the cherished memories we shared. To my beloved grandmother, Patricia Blue, your unwavering love and strength continue to shape my journey, a testament to the indomitable spirit of womanhood.

Kindred Spirits

In the tapestry of friendship, there are threads of gold woven by the hands of kindred spirits. To my dearest friend and confidant, Charvin "Chillz" - your friendship has been a lifeline in the tumultuous sea of life. From the playgrounds of youth to the trials of adulthood, your unwavering loyalty has been a beacon of hope in the darkest of nights.

A Heartfelt Farewell

To those who have gone before, leaving behind footprints in the sands of time, your memory remains etched in the annals of my heart. To my childhood friend, Robert Parler, your absence is a poignant reminder of life's fragility. Though parted by the veil of mortality, your spirit lives on in the cherished memories we shared.

A Symphony of Gratitude

In the symphony of life, each note is a testament to the indomitable human spirit. To my beloved Margaret "Peggy" Margie Bino Becker, your unwavering love and support have been the bedrock of my existence. Through the trials and tribulations, your steadfast presence has been a beacon of hope in the darkest of nights.

Epilogue: A Journey Unfolds

To those who have stood by me through thick and thin, your unwavering support has been a source of strength and inspiration. As I traverse the winding roads of life, I am filled with gratitude for the countless blessings that have paved the way. With each passing day, my love for you grows ever stronger, an unbreakable bond forged in the crucible of adversity.

1 THE POWER OF CHOICE

"Life is about choices. Some we regret, some we're proud of. Some will haunt us forever. The message is we are what we chose to be."
~Graham Brown

Life is a tapestry woven from the threads of our choices, each decision shaping the intricate design of our existence. From the moment we draw our first breath to the final beat of our hearts, we are confronted with an endless array of options, each one leading us down a different path. Some choices are made with clarity and conviction, while others are shrouded in doubt and uncertainty. Yet, regardless of the outcome, each decision leaves an indelible mark on the fabric of our lives, shaping who we are and who we become.

In the vast expanse of time, there exists a singular truth: we are what we choose to be. From the dawn of creation to the present moment, the universe has unfolded according to the choices made by its inhabitants. In the beginning, God spoke the word, and from that word, all things were formed. From the heavens above to the earth below, from the depths of the oceans to the heights of the mountains, every atom and molecule was brought into being through the power of choice.

As it is written in the book of Genesis, "In the beginning, God created the heavens and the earth." With a word, He spoke into existence the very fabric of reality, bringing order out of chaos and light out of darkness. And in the culmination of His creation, God formed man in His own image, breathing life into the dust of the earth and creating a companion to walk alongside Him in the garden of Eden.

Many millennia have passed since that fateful day, and yet the echoes of creation still reverberate throughout the cosmos. From the dust of the earth, God formed my ancestors, shaping their destinies and guiding their footsteps through the annals of history. And in the fullness of time, He brought forth my parents, uniting them in love and conceiving within them the spark of life that would one day become me.

I entered this world on a cool September morning, born into a family torn apart by addiction and strife. My father, a man of great potential and promise, was consumed by the demons of his past, while my mother, a woman of boundless love and compassion, struggled to break free from the shackles of her addiction. Together, they brought me into a world filled with pain and uncertainty, a world where the choices they made would shape the course of my life in ways I could scarcely imagine.

From the moment of my birth, I was marked by the consequences of their choices. Born with an addicted personality, I was predisposed to the same struggles that had plagued my parents for generations. And yet, even as a newborn babe, I was judged and stigmatized by the actions of those who came before me, labeled as a product of my environment and condemned to a fate not of my own making.

As I grew older, the weight of those expectations bore down upon me, shaping my identity and influencing the choices I would make. I was raised by my great grandmother, a woman of strength and resilience who instilled within me the values of hard work and determination. Yet, despite her best efforts, I could not escape the shadow of my past, nor the judgments of those who deemed me unworthy of love and acceptance.

From a young age, I felt the pull of the streets, drawn to the allure of a life filled with danger and excitement. I sought refuge in the camaraderie of my peers, finding solace in the brotherhood of those who shared my struggles and understood my pain. Together, we navigated the treacherous waters of adolescence, forging bonds that would withstand the test of time and trials.

But even as I embraced the life of the streets, I harbored dreams and aspirations that defied the expectations of those around me. I discovered a passion for music, a gift that allowed me to express myself and transcend the limitations of my circumstances. Yet, despite the undeniable talent that lay within me, I faced skepticism and doubt from those who believed that a better life was beyond my reach.

Determined to prove the naysayers wrong, I threw myself into my music, pouring my heart and soul into every lyric and melody. I believed that music was my ticket out of the streets, my ticket to a better life. Yet, even as I chased my dreams, I found myself ensnared by the very same traps that had ensnared my parents before me.

As I delved deeper into the world of music, I found myself drawn into a world of drugs and temptation. I sought refuge in the temporary highs and fleeting pleasures that substances provided, believing that they held the key to unlocking my full potential. Yet, even as I indulged in their embrace, I felt the weight of guilt and shame pressing down upon me, a constant reminder of the choices I had made and the consequences they wrought.

But amidst the darkness and despair, a glimmer of hope remained. I began to see glimpses of the man I could become; the man God had created me to be. I realized that true liberation could only be found through surrendering to a higher power, through acknowledging my own limitations and trusting in the divine plan that lay before me.

On December 4th, 2023, I made the choice to reclaim my life and surrender to the will of God. I entered into a program of recovery, seeking healing and redemption for the wounds that had long plagued me. And as I embarked on this journey of self-discovery and transformation, I found solace in the words of the psalmist, who wrote, "I will instruct you and teach you in the way you should go; I will counsel you with my loving eye on you."

With each passing day, I felt the burden of my past lifting from my shoulders, replaced by a sense of peace and purpose that I had long thought unattainable. I began to see the world through new eyes, to recognize the beauty and wonder that surrounded me on every side. And as I walked in the light of God's love, I knew that I was finally home.

Today, I stand as a testament to the power of choice and the transformative grace of God. I am no longer defined by the mistakes of my past, but rather by the choices I make in the present. I choose to walk in faith, to live with purpose, and to spread the message of hope and redemption to all who will listen.

Life is a journey of choices, and I am grateful for the opportunity to choose a path that leads to life and abundance. As I continue on this journey of faith and self-discovery, I am reminded of the words of Joshua, who said, "Choose this day whom you will serve... But as for me and my house, we will serve the Lord."

And so I choose, each and every day, to serve the Lord with all my heart, soul, and strength. For in Him, I find the strength to overcome every obstacle, the courage to face every challenge, and the hope to believe that a better tomorrow is within my grasp. And as I walk in His light, I know that I am truly free.

2 LIVE YOUR CHOICE

"Destiny is not a matter of chance; it is a matter of choice. It is not a thing to be waited for; it is a thing to be achieved." — William Jennings Bryan

For years, I was one of those individuals living on the edge, unsure of my dreams and aspirations, drifting along with the currents of life without a clear direction. I felt like a ship without a compass, tossed about by the winds of fate. But deep down, I knew I couldn't continue living this way forever. I had to take control of my destiny and chart my own course.

The turning point came when I realized that I had been living my life passively, waiting for something to happen to me rather than actively pursuing my goals. I knew that if I wanted to achieve my dreams, I had to make a choice to change my mindset and take decisive action.

So, I began by reflecting on what truly mattered to me and what I wanted to achieve in life. I took the time to identify my values, passions, and interests, which helped me gain clarity on my goals. With a clearer sense of direction, I made intentional choices aligned with my aspirations.

But living your choice isn't always easy. There were times when I faced obstacles and setbacks along the way. There were moments of doubt and uncertainty when I questioned whether I was on the right path. But in those moments, I reminded myself of William Jennings Bryan's quote that destiny is not a matter of chance but a matter of choice.

I realized that it was up to me to overcome these challenges and stay true to my vision. I had to persevere in the face of adversity and keep moving forward, one step at a time. And with each obstacle I overcame, I grew stronger and more determined to achieve my dreams.

Standing on my decisions was another important aspect of shaping my destiny. It meant having the courage to take risks and embrace failure as a stepping stone to success. It meant staying true to my values and not compromising my integrity for short term gains.

Sometimes, I faced criticism and opposition from others who didn't understand or support my choices. But I refused to let their negativity sway me from my path. Instead, I used their doubts as fuel to propel me forward, proving to myself and others that I was capable of achieving greatness.

And as I continued to live my choice and stand by my decisions, I began to see the fruits of my labor. I achieved goals that I once thought were impossible, and I discovered new passions and interests along the way. I realized that by taking control of my destiny, I had the power to create the life I had always dreamed of.

However, perhaps the most important lesson I learned on this journey is that destiny is not a destination but a journey. It's not about reaching a specific goal or milestone but about continuously evolving and growing as a person. It's about embracing the challenges and opportunities that come our way and using them to become the best version of ourselves.

So, if you ever find yourself feeling like your life is happening to you, remember that you have the power to shape your own destiny. It may not always be easy, and there will undoubtedly be obstacles along the way. But if you stay true to yourself and live with purpose and intention, there's no limit to what you can achieve.

In the vast landscape of life, where every decision, every action, and every moment hold the potential to shape our destiny, the guidance of mentors and the wisdom of experience become invaluable assets. For me, the words of my uncles, Ken and James Kinsey, echoed like a beacon of light, illuminating the path toward a life of purpose, excellence, and fulfillment.

"Ronnie, if you're going to do something, do it like a professional," my uncle James would often say, his voice carrying the weight of years of hard-earned wisdom. Those words became more than just advice; they became a mantra, a guiding principle that would shape my approach to life in ways I could never have imagined.

As a young boy growing up in Syracuse, New York, I was blessed with opportunities that many of my peers could only dream of. I had the privilege of being surrounded by mentors and coaches who believed in me, who saw potential where others saw obstacles, and who nurtured my talents with unwavering dedication.

Coach Ketorolac Lamar Earse, Coach Leon, Coach Kemp these were not just names on a roster; they were pillars of strength, sources of inspiration who taught me the value of discipline, determination, and hard work. Under their guidance, I learned that success was not a destination but a journey and that the road to greatness was paved with sacrifice and perseverance.

But it wasn't just on the field or the court where I learned the importance of living my choices. My uncles Ken and James Kinsey, both successful businessmen in their own right, imparted invaluable lessons that would shape my character and define my approach to life.

"Everything you do, do it like a professional," Uncle Ken would say, his voice brimming with authority and conviction. Whether it was pursuing my education, building a career, or nurturing relationships, his words served as a constant reminder of the importance of excellence in every endeavor.

And so, armed with the wisdom of my mentors and the guidance of my uncles, I set out on a journey to live my choices – to embrace the opportunities that life presented me with and to pursue my dreams with unwavering determination.

For me, living my choices meant more than just excelling in sports or academics; it meant making the right decisions that would set me on a path toward success and fulfillment. It meant resisting the temptations of the streets, staying focused on my goals, and never losing sight of the bigger picture.

But living my choices wasn't always easy. There were moments of doubt and uncertainty, times when the obstacles seemed insurmountable, and the road ahead appeared bleak. Yet, in those moments of darkness, I drew strength from the words of my mentors and the lessons of my uncles, knowing that adversity was simply a stepping stone on the path to greatness.

And so, I persevered. I woke up every day with a sense of purpose and gratitude, ready to tackle whatever challenges lay ahead. I set goals for myself – achievable, measurable goals that served as mile markers on the road to success. And I worked tirelessly, putting in the effort and dedication required to turn those goals into reality.

Living my choices meant having a plan of action and following through. It meant waking up every day grateful for another chance to win, another opportunity to take one step closer to becoming the best version of myself. It meant having a daily routine with structure and balance, not allowing chaos to dictate the course of my life.

And as I journeyed forth, I discovered that achieving my goals required more than just talent – it demanded unwavering commitment and perseverance. It meant being proactive rather than reactive and always striving to be the best version of myself.

Today, as I look back on my journey, I am grateful for the lessons I've learned and the people who have guided me along the way. My uncles Ken and James Kinsey, along with my coaches and mentors, have been instrumental in shaping my character and instilling in me the values of professionalism, dedication, and perseverance.

And as I continue to pursue my dreams and aspirations, I do so with the knowledge that my destiny is in my hands. By living my choices and striving for excellence in all that I do, I am confident that I can shape a future filled with success, fulfillment, and purpose.

The journey from darkness to light, from despair to redemption, is a tale as old as time – a narrative of triumph over adversity, of resilience in the face of hardship. And for me, that journey began with a simple realization: that the streets held nothing but emptiness and despair and that true fulfillment could only be found in the embrace of God's love and grace.

It took me years to come to this realization, years of making choices that I now look back on with regret and shame. Choices that led me down a path of self-destruction, choices that tore apart the very fabric of my being and left me adrift in a sea of addiction and despair.

But amidst the darkness, there were glimmers of light – voices of wisdom and guidance that called out to me, urging me to turn away from the path of destruction and embrace a life of purpose and meaning. One such voice belonged to a retired NBA referee, whose words echoed in my mind long after our encounter: "This block I'm risking my life for... if I go to jail for 25 years, it's still going to be here."

Those words struck a chord deep within me, awakening a sense of clarity and purpose that had long lay dormant. They reminded me that the streets held nothing but empty promises and shattered dreams and that true fulfillment could only be found in living a life aligned with God's plan for me.

But it wasn't until I hit rock bottom until I found myself standing on the precipice of despair, that I finally found the courage to confront my demons and seek help. It was at the White Deer Run rehabilitation center in Allenwood, Pennsylvania, that I began my journey toward healing and redemption.

There, surrounded by a community of kindred spirits and guided by mentors and counselors who believed in me when I could not believe in myself, I began to rebuild my life from the ground up. It was a journey fraught with challenges and setbacks, but through it all, I clung to the hope that, with God's grace, anything was possible.

My pastor Ike, whose unwavering faith and guidance helped me find my way back to God. My counselor, Jill, taught me the importance of self-love and self-worth. Ms. Shameka, whose tough love and unwavering support pushed me to confront the darkest corners of my soul. And Ms. Kim, whose kindness and wisdom reminded me of the strength and intelligence that lay within me.

But above all, it was the love and support of my newfound family at White Deer Run that sustained me through the darkest days of my journey. Their understanding and empathy, their willingness to walk alongside me as I navigated the treacherous waters of addiction and recovery, were a beacon of hope in a world consumed by darkness.

Today, as I stand on the threshold of a new chapter in my life, I am filled with a sense of gratitude and humility. Gratitude for the second chance that I have been given, for the opportunity to rebuild my life and reclaim my identity as a child of God. And humility in the knowledge that I am but one small part of a much larger story – a story of redemption and grace, of hope and healing.

As I look towards the future, I do so with a renewed sense of purpose and determination. No longer bound by the chains of addiction and despair, I am free to live a life that is aligned with God's plan for me – a life of righteousness, service, and love. And though the road ahead may be long and fraught with challenges, I walk it with confidence, knowing that I do not walk alone, for I am surrounded by a community of kindred spirits, mentors and friends who have walked this path before me and who continue to walk alongside me as I journey toward the light.

In the quiet of the morning, as the first rays of sunlight pierced through the darkness, I made a choice. Today, I chose not to let my past define me, not to allow the mistakes of yesterday to dictate the course of my tomorrow. Instead, I chose to harness the pain and the regret, the shame and the guilt, and use them as fuel to ignite a fire within me – a fire fueled not by anger or bitterness but by the unshakeable faith that only God can provide.

For me, faith is not just a belief; it is a way of life, a guiding light that illuminates the darkest corners of my soul. I believe in Yeshua, in Jesus Christ, and I trust in His plan for me. I have learned to relinquish control and surrender my desires and ambitions to a higher power, knowing that His plans are far greater than anything I could ever imagine.

As I sit in the passenger seat of life, with God at the wheel and faith by my side, I am filled with a sense of peace and contentment that I have never known before. I have learned to trust in the process, to embrace the journey, knowing that every twist and turn, every obstacle and challenge, is a stepping stone on the path to my destiny.

But faith alone is not enough; it must be accompanied by action. I have learned that in order to change the direction of my life, I must first change myself. I must confront the demons of my past, acknowledge the mistakes I have made, and commit to becoming the best version of myself.

And so, I have embarked on a journey of self-discovery and self-improvement, guided by the principles of love, kindness, and compassion. I have learned to love myself first, to value my time and the time of others, and to be mindful of the impact my actions have on those around me.

But perhaps most importantly, I have learned the power of dreaming – of daring to envision a life filled with purpose and meaning and then taking the necessary steps to turn that dream into reality. I have learned that with prayer, dedication, and determination, anything is possible.

It hasn't been easy. There have been moments of doubt and uncertainty, times when the weight of my past threatened to pull me back into the darkness. But I have learned to lean on my faith, to trust in God's plan, and to keep moving forward, one step at a time.

And as I look back on the journey that has brought me to this moment, I am filled with gratitude and humility. I am grateful for the second chance that I have been given, for the opportunity to rewrite the narrative of my life. And humility in the knowledge that I am but a small part of a much larger story – a story of redemption, of healing, and of hope.

So today, I choose to live my choice with a smile on my face and peace in my heart. I choose to be kind to others, to love myself enough to let go of negativity, and to embrace positivity. And I choose to walk in obedience to the Gospel, trusting in God's plan and His promises, knowing that He will never leave me nor forsake me.

Thank you, Father God, for being a God of understanding and healing. Thank you for guiding me out of darkness and into the light. As I continue on this journey, I ask for your continued protection and guidance, knowing that with you by my side, anything is possible.

Living with the choices we make delves deeper than merely accepting the consequences; it demands that we embrace them wholeheartedly, regardless of their implications. It beckons us to confront the essence of our being, to walk the path of integrity and purpose, guided by unwavering beliefs. Each decision, whether it leads us down a path of triumph or challenge, imprints its mark upon the canvas of our existence, shaping the very trajectory of our lives. It is incumbent upon us to not only accept these choices but to embody them with conviction, without yielding to the temptation of complaints.

In a world rife with blame and evasion, true strength emerges from the crucible of accountability. It calls upon us to confront our challenges with unyielding resolve, refusing to be shackled by the chains of excuses or self-pity. Instead of relinquishing control to external forces, we must seize the reins of our destiny, forging ahead with purpose and determination to craft the future we envision.

Yet, living with our choices transcends mere acquiescence; it compels us to revel in our victories and glean wisdom from our defeats. No achievement, however modest, should escape our acknowledgment, for each step forward, no matter how inconspicuous, propels us closer to our aspirations. By bestowing upon ourselves the recognition we deserve, we stoke the fires of motivation, propelling us forward in our pursuit of greatness.

Similarly, mistakes serve as the crucible of growth and evolution, offering invaluable lessons to those who dare to heed their teachings. Rather than succumbing to the weight of failure, we must embrace it as a catalyst for personal transformation. Through introspection and reflection, we discern the nuggets of wisdom concealed within our missteps, charting a course toward enlightenment and self-actualization.

Every choice we make reverberates with consequences, both auspicious and adverse, demanding that we confront their repercussions with equanimity. Whether basking in the glow of success or weathering the storm of adversity, it behooves us to assume responsibility for the impact our decisions wield upon our lives and the lives of others.

Life unfolds in fleeting moments, each one pregnant with the promise of possibility. Rather than languishing in the shadows of regret, we must seize the present with vigor and purpose, fashioning our destinies with intentionality and resolve. By infusing our choices with purposeful action, we harness the boundless potential of the present moment, birthing a future brimming with opportunity and promise.

Destiny, far from a capricious whim of fate, emerges as the culmination of our choices and actions. By committing wholeheartedly to our decisions and embracing both triumphs and tribulations, we sculpt our own destinies, crafting lives imbued with meaning and purpose. The power to effectuate change resides within us, eagerly awaiting activation through deliberate action and unyielding determination.

So, let us embark upon this journey with renewed fervor and determination, unearthing the treasures of opportunity that lie dormant within each and every moment. By living our choices with unwavering conviction and intentionality, we unlock the latent potential within us, ushering forth a future replete with fulfillment and accomplishment.

3 GETTING OUT YOUR OWN WAY

*"Get out of Your own way.
Often we're our own worst enemy
when working towards our goals."*
— *Robert T. Kiyosaki*

Ever find yourself caught in a loop of doubt and hesitation, like you're somehow your own worst enemy? It's a common struggle. I know because I've been there, stuck in a cycle of self-sabotage that seemed impossible to break. But here's the thing: you don't have to stay trapped in that pattern. You have the power to break free and chart your own path to success.

Let me share a bit of my own journey with you. There was a time when I constantly tripped myself up, held back by my own fears and insecurities. It wasn't until I reached out for support, sought guidance, and took decisive action that I began to see real progress. And guess what? You can do the same.

The first step? Recognizing the enemy within. It's those negative thoughts, that nagging self-doubt that likes to whisper in your ear and hold you back. But once you shine a light on those patterns, you can start to dismantle them one by one.

But here's the secret weapon: you don't have to go it alone. Seriously, asking for help is not a sign of weakness it's a sign of strength. Whether it's finding a mentor who's been there, hiring a coach to keep you accountable, or simply leaning on a trusted friend for support, having someone in your corner can make all the difference.

So, let's flip the script. Instead of staying stuck in the same old patterns, let's break free and start living the life we've always dreamed of. It's time to silence that inner critic and step boldly into the future we deserve. And remember, you've got a whole team of supporters cheering you on every step of the way.

Are you tired of feeling like you're constantly tripping over your own feet on the road to success? Trust me, I've been there. But here's the thing: you don't have to keep getting in your own way. With a little help from some friends (and a dash of determination), you can kick those self-sabotaging habits to the curb and start making real progress toward your goals.

So, how do we do it? Well, it starts with getting clear on what you want. Setting intentions is like drawing a map it gives you direction and purpose. Once you know where you're headed, it's time to plot your course. Creating a solid plan of action helps keep you on track and gives you something to lean on when the going gets tough.

But hey, let's not forget the power of mindset. Cultivating a positive outlook can work wonders. And don't skimp on the self-care either. Taking time to recharge your batteries and nurture your spirit is key to staying resilient in the face of challenges.

Now, I won't lie to you breaking free from those self-imposed limitations isn't always easy. Fear and self-doubt can be stubborn little monsters. But here's the secret: you've got what it takes to slay them. With a little bit of grit and a whole lot of heart, you can push past those obstacles and reach for the stars.

So, what are you waiting for? It's time to stop letting fear call the shots and start living the life you've always dreamed of. You've got the power within you to make it happen. So go ahead, take that first step. The journey may be challenging, but trust me, the view from the top is oh-so sweet.

In today's whirlwind of a world, it's all too easy to fall into the trap of thinking we have to handle everything on our own. We've crafted this narrative that asking for help is a sign of weakness, a crack in the façade of our self-sufficiency. We've been conditioned to believe that we should be able to navigate life's labyrinthine challenges independently, armed with nothing but our own grit and determination. But here's the thing: this rugged individualism, while admirable in its own right, often leaves us feeling like we're drowning in a sea of responsibilities, overwhelmed, stuck, and utterly isolated.

It's time for a paradigm shift, a revolution in the way we perceive our own limitations and capabilities. It's time to break free from the shackles of the belief that we have to go it alone. Instead, let's embrace the radical notion that we are not the problem; we are the solution. It's about recognizing that there is strength in vulnerability, power in collaboration.

Picture this: you're standing at a crossroads, weighed down by the burdens of life's trials and tribulations. You could continue to trudge along the solitary path, shouldering the weight of the world on your own weary shoulders. Or, you could take a leap of faith, reaching out for the helping hand that's been waiting patiently by your side all along. It's a choice between stagnation and transformation, between isolation and connection.

Making the decision to seek help is an act of profound courage, a bold declaration of your commitment to your own growth and well-being. It's about acknowledging that, despite your best efforts, you don't have all the answers and that's perfectly okay. It's about letting go of the ego-driven notion that asking for assistance somehow diminishes your worth. In fact, it's quite the opposite: by relinquishing your pride and embracing the support of others, you create space for new possibilities to emerge, for serendipitous encounters and unforeseen opportunities to take root and flourish.

So, the next time you find yourself at a crossroads, paralyzed by indecision or overwhelmed by the weight of the world, remember this: you are not alone. There is a vast network of support waiting to buoy you up and propel you forward on your journey. All you have to do is reach out and take that first, courageous step toward the transformative power of collaboration.

Imagine this: you're standing at the edge of the train tracks, the rumble of an oncoming locomotive echoing in the distance. It's a metaphorical crossroads, a moment frozen in time where the decisions you make will shape your destiny. There are no physical barriers holding you in place, no external forces compelling you to stay. It's just you, alone with your thoughts, facing down the imminent threat of the approaching train.

In this moment, you realize something profound: despite the overwhelming power of the train hurtling toward you, you are the one in control. You have the power to choose whether to stand your ground or to take decisive action and step aside. It's a choice between stagnation and movement, between surrender and empowerment.

But here's the twist: the real challenge isn't the train itself it's the battle raging within. It's the voice in your head that whispers doubt and fear, the invisible force that holds you back from stepping into your true potential. Ever felt like you're trying to outrun your own shadow, only to realize that no matter where you go, you're still there, haunting your every move?

It's a sobering realization: if we hadn't created the mess in the first place, we wouldn't be scrambling to escape it. Instead, we'd be charging forward with purpose and clarity, fueled by the fire of our dreams. We'd be sprinting toward success, leaving the darkness behind as we race toward the light.

But here's the thing about light: it's not just a destination; it's a journey. And sometimes, the path to enlightenment requires us to relinquish the illusion of control, to surrender to a higher power and trust in the guidance of the universe. It's about recognizing that we are not alone, that there is a divine plan unfolding before us, if only we have the courage to follow it.

So, the next time you find yourself standing in the path of an oncoming train whether metaphorical or literal remember this: you are the master of your fate. You have the power to get out of your own way, to step into the fullness of your potential, and to embrace the journey that awaits.

Devorn's words, (one of my cousin) "Cuzzz you in the way Cuzzz," echoed in my mind for years, shaping my outlook on life. For so long, I found myself trapped in a cycle of self-sabotage, blaming external factors for my lack of progress. At 18, 25, even at 30, I felt like I was stuck, unable to break free from the limitations I had imposed upon myself.

Despite my talent and intelligence, I squandered the gifts I had been blessed with, choosing instead to blend in when I was meant to stand out. It's a common struggle we're torn between the desire to conform and the call to greatness. Some of us are born to lead, while others fall into the role of follower, easily swayed by the currents of society.

I'll admit, I was one of the ones who got swept away. I wanted to belong, to be a part of something bigger than myself, even if it meant sacrificing my true purpose. But deep down, I knew I was meant for more. I was meant to lead, to inspire, to uplift.

It took a wake-up call from Ms. Kim at White Deer Run to set me straight. She saw the potential in me, even when I couldn't see it in myself. And slowly but surely, I began to realize that I was the only one standing in my own way.

But breaking free from old habits is easier said than done. It's a journey filled with ups and downs, moments of strength and moments of weakness. That's why I turn to God and my counselor for guidance, seeking solace and clarity in times of uncertainty.

It's a process, a journey of self-discovery and self-improvement. But with each step forward, I feel myself getting closer to fulfilling my true purpose to lead others out of the darkness and into the light. And for that, I am eternally grateful.

For years, I struggled to fit into a mold that wasn't meant for me. I chased after false ideals, trying to emulate someone else's version of success instead of embracing my own uniqueness. But the truth is, it's exhausting trying to be someone you're not, especially when the world is already full of imitations.

Eventually, I reached a breaking point. I couldn't ignore the weight of my own failures any longer. It was like a light bulb moment, a sudden realization that there had to be more to life than this endless cycle of disappointment and disillusionment. I yearned for something greater, something that would fulfill me in a way that chasing after superficial goals never could.

It was in that moment of desperation that I had a spiritual awakening. It was like God was knocking on the door of my heart, waiting patiently for me to finally open it and let Him in. And when I did, everything changed.

It wasn't easy, of course. Making the decision to surrender control and let God take the wheel required a level of courage and humility that I hadn't known before. It meant facing my own shortcomings head-on, owning up to my mistakes, and being brutally honest with myself and those around me.

But with every step I took toward surrender, I felt a weight lift off my shoulders. It was like I was finally coming home to myself, rediscovering who I was meant to be all along. And as I began to align my life with God's plan for me, I found a sense of peace and purpose that I had never known before.

It's a journey, to be sure one filled with ups and downs, moments of joy and moments of pain. But through it all, I know that I'm exactly where I'm supposed to be. And that's the beauty of surrendering to God's will it's not about giving up control, but rather gaining true freedom and fulfillment.

It's a harsh reality check when you look around and realize that everyone you grew up with seems to be living their best life while you're still stuck in the same old rut. They're flaunting their new cars, splurging on the latest sneakers, jetting off on vacations, and unlocking the door to their swanky new apartments. Meanwhile, you're left feeling like you're driving in circles, going nowhere fast. I know that feeling all too well it's been my reality for far too many years.

But here's the thing: this is where all those well-meaning words of advice from friends and family start to hit home. It's a wake-up call, a nudge from the universe urging us to take stock of our lives and make some much-needed changes. And it all starts with a little soul cleansing, a journey inward to heal and transform from the inside out.

For me, that meant letting God in, allowing Him to reshape my heart and mind from the inside out. And let me tell you, the transformation was nothing short of miraculous. It wasn't about flashy clothes or trendy accessories—it was about radiating a genuine inner peace and contentment that no amount of material wealth could ever buy.

But getting out of your own way isn't just about a spiritual awakening it's about taking concrete steps to improve your mental and physical well-being. It might mean seeking counseling to work through past traumas, or finally committing to a healthier lifestyle by hitting the gym and cleaning up your diet.

And let's not forget the importance of carving out time for silence and solitude, away from the constant buzz of notifications and distractions. It's in those quiet moments of reflection that we can truly connect with God and find clarity amidst the chaos of daily life.

So, whether it's diving into self-help literature, tuning into motivational speeches, or simply taking a moment to breathe and recalibrate, getting out of your own way is a journey worth embarking on—one that leads not just to outward success, but to inner peace and fulfillment.

Truly surrendering to a power greater than ourselves and seeking guidance from those who embody righteousness and wisdom is when the real journey of transformation begins. It's a pivotal moment, a turning point where we finally start to live life authentically, guided by a higher purpose.

But let's be real it's not a walk in the park. It takes time, prayer, and a willingness to embrace solitude in order to discern the path that God has laid out for us. And yes, it requires hard work a dedication to self-improvement and a commitment to growth that can't be taken lightly.

I remember hearing a powerful lesson in my Narcotics Anonymous meetings: addiction is about losing everything for one thing, while recovery is about giving up one thing to gain everything. It's a profound truth that applies not just to those struggling with substance abuse, but to anyone grappling with life's challenges.

When we get out of our own way, when we relinquish control and surrender to a higher power, we open ourselves up to a world of possibilities. It's a journey of self-discovery and self-renewal, where we shed the layers of our old selves and emerge as stronger, wiser individuals.

So, yes, it's tough. It's a battle waged on multiple fronts, against our own demons and the external forces that seek to hold us back. But the rewards are immeasurable. As we shed the shackles of self-doubt and insecurity, as we embrace our true selves and align our lives with God's plan, we find a sense of peace and fulfillment that surpasses anything we could have imagined.

So, don't be discouraged by the challenges that lie ahead. Embrace them as opportunities for growth and transformation. Because when you get out of your own way, when you surrender to the divine guidance that surrounds you, that's when your life truly begins to flourish.

Absolutely, the journey to a new life begins with a willingness to change and a commitment to developing healthier habits and thought patterns. It's about taking those initial steps towards self-improvement, knowing that this is just the beginning of a transformative journey.

I've come to understand that this journey is not about reaching a specific destination it's about embracing the process and staying true to the path laid out before us. With a clear roadmap and unwavering determination, anything is possible.

It's a shift in mindset, a recognition that the same energy we once poured into destructive behaviors can be redirected towards positive growth and fulfillment. Whether it's hitting the gym to strengthen our bodies or deepening our connection with God through prayer and worship, the key is consistency and dedication.

And let's not forget the importance of relationships both with our loved ones and with our higher power. Being present and attentive in our children's lives, listening to our parents' guidance no matter our age these are all vital components of getting out of our own way and embracing the wisdom of others.

So, as we embark on this journey of self-discovery and transformation, let's remember *that change is possible, one step at a time.* It's about being open to guidance, being willing to put in the effort, and trusting in the process. And with each small victory, we move closer to the life we've always dreamed of a life lived with purpose, fulfillment, and joy.

Absolutely, transitioning to a better life demands an equal if not greater level of effort than what we once exerted in our old ways. It's a lesson that took me far too long to grasp, but I've come to realize that it's better to bloom late than to never blossom at all.

Sometimes, it's essential to relinquish control and take a backseat, allowing someone else to steer the ship. This shift in perspective offers clarity, allowing us to see the world through fresh eyes and appreciate its beauty from a different angle.

Getting out of our own way doesn't mean relinquishing control of our lives entirely it simply means acknowledging that we don't have all the answers. It's about recognizing when we need guidance and being open to receiving it from others. Just think about our parents navigating long road trips without the aid of GPS technology relying on paper maps and trusting in the guidance of strangers. It required faith, focus, and a willingness to adapt to the journey ahead.

But getting out of our own way also requires faith a belief in something greater than ourselves and the conviction that we are worthy of change. It's about understanding our past, envisioning our future, and having the courage to release the wheel and let God take control.

So, I urge you: let go of the wheel, step aside, and allow the miracle of transformation to unfold. Don't lose faith when blessings are within reach. All it takes is a willingness to get out of our own way. So, ask yourself: are you ready to make that leap today? Once you find the answer, the journey towards change can truly begin as long as that answer is yes.

Getting out of your own way is about embracing a shift in perspective one that acknowledges that your past mistakes don't define your future. It's about believing in yourself today, despite the doubts and insecurities that may linger.

Mentally getting out of your own way means actively changing your thought patterns and habits. It's about being mindful of the content you consume, the company you keep, and seeking help when needed.

Emotionally getting out of your own way involves confronting your feelings and letting go of past hurts. It's about releasing the burdens that weigh you down and surrendering to a higher power.

Physically getting out of your own way starts with taking care of your body exercising regularly, eating nutritious foods, and prioritizing self-care.

Financially getting out of your own way requires learning about money management, budgeting, and saving for the future.

Spiritually getting out of your own way means aligning yourself with a higher purpose and using your talents for the greater good.

Ultimately, getting out of your own way is a choice a decision to live better, to strive for growth, and to embrace the possibilities that lie ahead. It's about taking that first step towards a brighter future, knowing that you deserve it and that change is possible.

When we find the courage to open up and ask for help, it's like unlocking a door to a world of compassion and understanding. It's reaching out to someone a *mentor*, a *friend*, or a *therapist* and saying, "*I need you*," and feeling the weight of the world lift off our shoulders, if only for a moment.

The truth is, we weren't designed to go it alone. We're wired for connection, for those moments of shared vulnerability and shared strength that bind us together. And when we embrace that truth, when we lean into it and allow ourselves to be supported, amazing things can happen.

Asking for help isn't a sign of weakness; it's a sign of bravery. It's acknowledging that we don't have all the answers, that we're not perfect, and that's okay. It's saying, "I'm struggling, but I'm willing to reach out and let someone in."

I've learned that the key to a truly fulfilling life lies in our ability to connect with others, to let them in and share our burdens and our joys. It's about understanding that we're all in this together, navigating the twists and turns of life's journey side by side.

So, let's take that first step together. Let's reach out, ask for help, and allow ourselves to be supported. Because when we do, we open ourselves up to a world of possibilities a world where anything is possible, and where we can truly thrive.

We all hold onto dreams of a brighter future, yet sometimes, we're trapped in patterns that drag us down. It's time to break free, to take that first brave step toward a better tomorrow by reaching out for help and embracing the support of those around us.

Before we can move forward, we need to face the demons holding us back—the negative self-talk, the fear of failure, the habits that keep us stuck. It's about acknowledging these struggles, understanding how they weigh us down, and committing to breaking free from their grip.

Let's stop standing in our own way, blocking our own path to success. Whether it's self-doubt gnawing at our confidence, the relentless pursuit of perfection that leaves us paralyzed, or the fear of change that holds us back, it's time to let go. It's time to release the limiting beliefs and behaviors that keep us from reaching our full potential.

It won't be easy, but it's a journey worth taking. As we shed these burdens, we open ourselves up to new possibilities, new horizons, and a future filled with promise. So let's be brave, let's be vulnerable, and let's ask for help. Together, we can break free and pave the way for a brighter, more fulfilling tomorrow.

Asking for help isn't a sign of weakness; it's a testament to our strength and courage. It's about shedding the notion that we must navigate life's challenges solo and instead, opening ourselves up to the support of others. Whether it's seeking guidance from a mentor, confiding in a therapist, or leaning on friends and family, there's immense power in reaching out for assistance. By embracing the support of others, we invite fresh perspectives, insights, and resources into our lives, propelling us forward on the path to a brighter future.

At times, we all find ourselves grappling with obstacles that seem insurmountable. In those moments, seeking guidance from a trusted coach, counselor, or spiritual advisor can provide invaluable clarity and direction. Their wisdom and expertise can illuminate our path, empowering us to make informed decisions and take meaningful strides toward our goals.

So, let's take that pivotal first step toward a brighter tomorrow. Let's cast aside self-destructive patterns, relinquish the burden of going it alone, and lean into the wisdom and support of those around us. Together, we can forge a future filled with hope, possibility, and joy. It's time to step out of our own way and bask in the radiance of a tomorrow filled with promise.

In our pursuit of a brighter future, we often find ourselves hindered by self-destructive patterns.

However, by acknowledging our limitations and seeking help from mentors, therapists, and loved ones, we

unlock the strength and courage to overcome obstacles.

Embracing support propels us toward growth, offering new perspectives and resources to navigate life's

challenges. Let's shed self-imposed barriers, embrace the wisdom of others, and step boldly into a future filled with hope and possibility.

4 TRUTH BE TOLD

"Courage is telling the truth when a lie would be easier."
~Unknown

In many human experiences, courage often appears in grand, heroic acts, such as bravely confronting danger. However, hidden within these impressive displays is a quieter but equally powerful courage, the bravery to accept and speak the truth, even when it may be easier to hide behind lies. In a world of deception, honesty symbolizes change, offering freedom, personal development, healing, and liberty.

"The truth will set you free" is a timeless saying that resonates throughout human wisdom. Its impact reaches into every aspect of our lives. When we dare to be honest with ourselves and others, we free ourselves from falsehoods and deception. Living authentically becomes a decision and a release, leading the way to inner peace and genuine freedom.

However, truth, despite its liberating appeal, can be a double-edged sword. It reveals our flaws and mistakes, cutting through illusions. For Jacob, a recovering addict, facing the truth meant recognizing the depths of his addiction and the pain it caused his loved ones. It was a harsh truth to accept, yet he found the first glimmer of hope, the chance for redemption and to carve out a new path forward in that raw honesty.

The pursuit of living with truthfulness is not for the weakhearted. It requires confronting our deepest fears and facing our past errors honestly. However, this bravery sets us free from the bonds of falsehood, allowing us to traverse the world with genuineness as our guiding star.

For many, faith is intricately woven into the fabric of honesty. Relying on a higher power brings comfort in times of uncertainty, infusing our challenges with significance and purpose. During quiet prayer or meditation moments, we find the resilience to navigate life's turbulent waters with integrity as our guide.

Nevertheless, the path of honesty is filled with obstacles, its terrain rough and harsh. Yet, the rewards are limitless for those daring enough to walk it. Embracing a life of truth leads to discovering freedom, transcending earthly limitations, and peace surpassing comprehension. Along our journey, we become sources of inspiration, shining light on the shadows of dishonesty and inviting others to embrace authenticity.

Ultimately, it comes down to faith in ourselves and the power of honesty to transform lives and reshape worlds. When we ground ourselves in this faith, we become creators of our destiny, forging paths of fulfillment and purpose. And in our wake, we leave behind a legacy, a world illuminated by the luminosity of truth, where bravery reigns supreme and authenticity is the catalyst for change.

A shared thread links us all in the fabric of our lives: the pursuit of truth, the path toward living genuinely, and the aspiration to motivate others along the journey. In telling our narratives, victories, and setbacks, we find the bravery to be boldly truthful, paving the way for personal development and satisfaction.

There's Jacob, whose pursuit of truth was forged in the crucible of addiction and personal renewal. His journey was marked by dark paths and obscure corners where the enticement of escape tempted him. However, in the depths of despair, Jacob found a glimmer of hope, a faith that transcended his past errors and offered him an opportunity for redemption. Through his trials and victories, Jacob became an inspiration, demonstrating to others that there's always a route back to the light, no matter how far we've veered.

Yet, honesty is not only about confronting external struggles; it's also about facing our internal demons with unyielding bravery. For me, that journey began in the shadows of a fractured childhood, where the absence of parental affection left me feeling lost. Seeking a sense of belonging, I wandered down shadowy paths, seeking comfort in a group and finding solace in the numbing embrace of substances. Yet, through the agony and the tears, I discovered a wellspring of resilience I never knew I possessed – a resilience nurtured by forgiveness, self-care, and the steadfast belief that redemption is always attainable.

Ultimately, our stories are not just accounting of hardship and renewal; they are testimonials of the power of honesty, the strength of the human spirit, and the transformative potential of faith. They remind us that no matter how dark the night may seem, there's always a glimmer of light on the horizon waiting to guide us home. So let us walk confidently in the path of truth, motivating others with our bravery and illuminating a brighter, more genuine future.

Picture a child lost in the vast expanse of a world that seems too big and daunting for their small frame to navigate alone. That was me, a little soul adrift in a sea of loneliness, longing for the warmth of familial love that seemed forever out of reach.

In the depths of my despair, I found solace in the company of a gang. Oh, the allure of belonging! I thought I had finally found my tribe, my place to call home amidst the world's chaos. But little did I know, I was stepping into a whirlwind of trouble, a storm that would sweep me up and toss me around like a rag doll.

With each passing day, I found myself entangled in a web of criminality, a tangled mess of lies and deceit that threatened to suffocate me. But it was too late to turn back; I had taken the plunge, diving headfirst into a world of danger and desperation.

And then came the drugs, my sweet escape from the harsh realities of life. Oh, how they whispered promises of oblivion, of temporary respite from the pain that gnawed at my soul. But oh, the price I paid! Each hit was a nail in the coffin of my innocence, each pill a step closer to my demise.

As the years rolled by, I found myself shackled by the chains of addiction, a slave to my desires. What started as innocent curiosity soon morphed into a voracious hunger, an insatiable thirst for oblivion that consumed me whole.

Living Authentically and Courageously

And so, I turned to theft, a desperate bid to fuel my addiction and silence the demons that haunted my every waking moment. I stole from those closest to me, betraying their trust in a futile attempt to satisfy the cravings that ravaged my soul.

But even as I filled my pockets with ill-gotten gains, I found no solace, no peace of mind. Instead, I was left with nothing but guilt and shame, my heart heavy with the weight of my sins.

Yet, in the depths of my despair, a glimmer of hope flickered, a tiny flame fighting to stay alight amidst the darkness. And it was in that moment, that fragile spark of hope, I found the strength to rise from the ashes of my past and forge a new path forward.

In the depths of my soul, I carried a heavy burden, the weight of my sins pressing down on me like a leaden shroud. Each day, as I strayed further from the path of righteousness, I felt the sting of guilt gnawing at my conscience, a constant reminder of my wayward ways.

But it took a moment of divine intervention, a spark of clarity amidst the chaos of my life, for me to finally confront the truth of my actions. With trembling hands and a quivering heart, I knelt before God, ready to bare my soul and confess my sins.

Oh, the anguish of that confession! It required me to peel back the layers of deceit and betrayal to expose the raw truth of my transgressions. Yet, amid my vulnerability, I found a glimmer of hope, a beacon of light shining through the darkness of my despair.

As I poured out my heart to God, I felt a weight lift from my shoulders, a burden I had carried for far too long. In its place, I felt a sense of peace wash over me, a peace that could only come from the divine forgiveness of my Creator.

With God's grace as my guiding light, I embarked on a journey of redemption and renewal. I sought help for my addiction, leaning on my faith, my family, and my community for support. It was a journey fraught with challenges and obstacles, but with each step forward, I felt the warmth of God's love enveloping me like a comforting embrace.

Through it all, I came to a profound realization that forgiveness is not just an act of mercy bestowed upon others but a gift we give ourselves. By releasing the resentment I harbored toward my parents, I liberated myself from the chains of anger and bitterness, embracing a newfound sense of peace and acceptance.

Let me tell you a story of gratitude, resilience, and the transformative power of redemption. It's a tale of trials and triumphs, of finding light in the darkest of nights and emerging stronger, wiser, and more compassionate than ever before.

Imagine this: an individual's spirit, battered and bruised by life's harsh and unpredictable challenges, yet resiliently standing upright amidst the ruins. That spirit belongs to me, shaped in the fiery furnace of hardship and strengthened through the tests encountered on my path.

Through the haze of depression and despair, I stumbled and fell, grappling with demons that threatened to consume me whole. But in my darkest hour, I found a flicker of hope, a glimmer of light piercing the shadows and whispering of brighter days.

It was a journey of self-discovery, of learning to love and accept myself, flaws and all. Through the tears and the turmoil, I found solace in the knowledge that my struggles were not in vain – they were the building blocks of my strength, the stepping stones to my salvation.

And oh, the power of forgiveness! It was a balm for my wounded soul, a salve that soothed the ache of past hurts and grievances. In forgiving others, I found freedom from the chains of resentment and bitterness that had bound me for so long.

But perhaps the greatest gift of all was the gift of faith, a faith that sustained me through the darkest of nights and guided me toward the light of a new dawn. With God by my side, I faced my demons head-on, confronting my addiction, my sins, and my shortcomings with courage and humility.

Though the road was long and fraught with challenges, I emerged victorious, a beacon of hope for those who still walk in darkness, a testament to the power of redemption and grace.

So let us all take heart in the knowledge that no matter how far we may fall, redemption is always within reach. Let us find strength in our struggles, courage in our convictions, and hope for a brighter tomorrow. Ultimately, it is not our past that defines us but our journey towards a better, brighter future.

A Raw Journey Through Addiction

Let me take you on a journey through the shadows of my past, where desperation and addiction danced hand in hand, leading me down a treacherous path of self-destruction. Brace yourself for a raw and unfiltered account of how I plunged headfirst into the abyss of drug addiction, heedless of the wreckage I left in my wake.

It all began in the innocence of youth, a time when I was ripe for the picking, vulnerable to the siren call of drugs and the intoxicating allure of risky thrills. Little did I know that my flirtation with pleasure would soon morph into a full blown obsession, a voracious hunger that consumed me whole.

As my addiction tightened its grip around my soul, I found myself descending into a dark and twisted realm where morality held no sway. I became a slave to my cravings, willing to do whatever it took to satiate the insatiable hunger gnawing at my insides.

Oh, the lengths I went to feed my addiction! I manipulated and deceived those closest to me, weaving a tangled web of lies and deceit in my desperate quest for another hit. I betrayed their trust without a second thought, blind to the pain and anguish I was causing.

And as the consequences of my actions piled up around me like a mountain of rubble, I remained steadfast in my self-destructive ways. I engaged in reckless and dangerous behavior, heedless of the risks and the wreckage I left in my wake.

But even as I hurtled toward rock bottom, I remained blind to the devastation I was wreaking upon myself and those around me. I finally saw the light when I stared into the abyss, teetering on the brink of oblivion.

So join me as I navigate the labyrinth of addiction and redemption, a journey fraught with danger and despair but also marked by moments of grace and hope. In the darkness of my past lies a glimmer of light, a beacon of hope for those still lost in the shadows.

Imagine a solitary spirit lost amidst the waves of darkness, tossed by the storms of addiction and hopelessness. It was my tumultuous creation, my soul weary and wounded by the burden of my wrongdoings.

But amidst the chaos and the deafening roar of my self-destruction, I heard a whisper of hope, redemption, and divine grace. It was the voice of God, calling out to me from the depths of my despair, offering me a lifeline in my darkest hour.

With trembling hands and a quivering heart, I reached out to Him, ready to surrender to His mercy and love. In that moment of surrender, I felt a shift, a change of heart, a stirring of the soul that set me on a path toward healing and redemption.

Oh, the power of God's grace! It washed over me like a gentle tide, soothing the wounds of my past and lighting the way towards a brighter tomorrow. With each step I took on this newfound path of righteousness, I felt the burdens of my past slipping away, replaced by a sense of peace and purpose that I had never known before.

And so, with a heart full of gratitude and a renewed spirit, I boldly decided to leave behind the shackles of my old life and embrace a new way of being a life of sobriety, healing, and faith.

But the journey toward redemption was not without its challenges. I had to learn to forgive myself for my past mistakes and let go of the shame and guilt that had weighed me down for so long. Through the grace of God, I found the strength to embrace my humanity, flaws and all, and turn my gaze toward the future with hope and optimism.

From Darkness to Light

Now, as I stand before you, a living testament to the transformative power of God's love, I hope to inspire others struggling with addiction or destructive habits. Know this: your past does not define you, and with the love and grace of God, you can overcome any obstacle in your path.

So take heart, my friends, and trust in God's plan for you. Allow His love to guide you towards a brighter, more fulfilling future, and know that redemption is always within reach no matter how far you have strayed.

Imagine a journey from the depths of despair to the soaring heights of self-discovery and purpose. That's the story of my life, a tale of transformation from follower to the natural-born leader that God always intended me to be.

Growing up without a father and siblings left me adrift in a sea of loneliness, desperately searching for love and belonging. And where did I turn to fill that void? The streets were a harsh and unforgiving landscape that promised everything I lacked at home.

But oh, the price I paid for seeking solace in the streets! From the tender age of 12 until my 26th year, I walked a path fraught with danger and despair. Heartache became my constant companion, physical wounds my badge of honor, and the stigma of gang membership my burden to bear.

Each day and night were battles to survive in a world that seemed determined to swallow me whole. But through the haze of pain and regret, I caught glimpses of a higher purpose, a divine plan unfolding before my eyes.

And it was in the throes of addiction, in the darkest moments of my life, that I felt the gentle touch of God's grace. His mercy lifted me from the depths of despair, His love that healed the wounds of my past, and His guidance that set me on a new path of self-discovery and redemption.

Now, as I stand on the precipice of a new beginning, I am grateful for the journey that brought me here, for it is through my pain that I have found purpose, through my struggles that I have discovered strength, and through my mistakes that I have learned the true meaning of grace.

So, let my story be a beacon of hope for those who walk in darkness, a testament to the power of faith and redemption. No matter how lost or broken we may feel, there is always a path forward, a chance for renewal and transformation. And it all begins with a single step, taken in faith and guided by the hand of a loving God.

Embracing a New Identity

As I journey through the winding roads of self-discovery, I am enveloped in the comforting embrace of my identity as a cherished child of God. This revelation fills me with a profound sense of peace and purpose as I learn to surrender to His divine plan for my life.

Overcoming the Past

Gone are the days when I allowed my past mistakes to define me, shackling me to a narrative of shame and regret. Now, I stand tall in the knowledge that I am a new creation fashioned by the loving hands of my Creator. With each step forward, I feel the weight of my burdens lifting, replaced by God's boundless grace and forgiveness.

No longer content to merely follow in the footsteps of others, I now stride confidently forward as a leader in God's kingdom. It's a role I never imagined for myself, but one that I embrace wholeheartedly, knowing His unwavering love and wisdom guide me.

Weathering Life's Storms

Through the storms of addiction and toxic relationships, I weathered the tempest with unwavering faith, clinging to the promise of brighter days ahead. And though I lost some along the way – friends who could not bear the weight of my journey and family members who faltered in their support I gained so much more in their absence.

Finding Strength in Faith

For in the void left by those who could not walk alongside me, God brought forth new friendships and opportunities for growth that surpassed my wildest dreams. It was a reminder that even in our darkest moments, His light shines brightest, illuminating the path to healing and redemption.

And so, with each passing day, I find myself letting go of the toxic relationships that once held me back, releasing them to the care of a loving God who knows what is best for me. It's a bittersweet farewell that paves the way for new beginnings and fresh growth opportunities.

Ultimately, I am reminded that the past is a stepping stone on the journey to our true selves and that anything is possible with God by our side. So let us trust in His plan, embrace our identities as leaders in His kingdom, and journey forth with courage and conviction, knowing He is always guiding us toward a brighter tomorrow.

Through the haze of my struggles, I began to discern the true friends that God had strategically placed in my life. They weren't just acquaintances but my pillars of support, encouragers, and accountability partners. Through their unwavering presence, they helped me navigate the stormy seas of recovery, guiding me toward the light at the end of the tunnel.

Embracing Honesty

With God as my anchor, I found the strength to break free from the suffocating grip of addiction. It was a battle fraught with temptation and trials, but I emerged victorious through the power of the Holy Spirit coursing through my veins. Each day was a testament to His grace, a testament to the freedom and purpose that awaited me on the other side of addiction's chains.

But honesty, ah, that was the key that unlocked the door to true healing. It wasn't just about being truthful with others but confronting my soul's raw, unfiltered truth. No more hiding behind masks of self-deception or denial. It was time to face my inner demons and acknowledge my mistakes, regrets, and deepest wounds.

And so, armed with courage and humility, I embarked on a journey of self-discovery and forgiveness. I repented for my sins, confessed my wrongdoings, and sought forgiveness from those I hurt. It was a cathartic process, a shedding of the past that paved the way for a brighter, more hopeful future.

But let me tell you, honesty is not always gentle or diplomatic. Sometimes, it's a brutal reckoning with the harsh realities of life. It's about tearing down the walls of falsehood and illusion, exposing the tender underbelly of our humanity. And though it may be uncomfortable, even painful at times, it is essential for growth and transformation.

So, let us embrace honesty with open arms, my friends, for it is the gateway to true freedom and fulfillment. Let us face our truths, both light and shadow, with courage and conviction, knowing that in doing so, we pave the way for a future filled with healing, wholeness, and grace.

As I journey down the winding road of recovery, I lift my prayers to the heavens, praying to God for the growth and deepening of my relationship with my fiancé. But should our paths diverge, I surrender to His divine wisdom, trusting that He will lead me to a God-fearing woman who will walk beside me in unwavering faith and love, for I believe that in God's grand design, marriage, and family are integral parts of my future, destined to bloom in His perfect timing. With His guiding hand, I am certain I can break free from the shadows of dysfunction, weaving a tapestry of love and faith that will echo through the generations.

Through the storm of addiction and toxic relationships, I have emerged anew, cradled in the embrace of God's boundless love. I no longer dwell in the shadows of my past; instead, I bask in the radiant light of purpose and fulfillment. Each day brings new blessings and true friendships, a testament to God's unwavering grace and mercy in my life. With Him by my side, I am encouraged to face any challenge that may come my way, knowing that His strength is my anchor and His love is my shield.

A Path to Healing and Freedom

Thank God for His boundless grace, for it is through His mercy that I find the courage to speak with unwavering conviction and unyielding honesty. For courage, my friends, is not merely about braving external challenges but also about confronting the truths that lie dormant within our souls. It is about peeling back the layers of deception and self-deception, allowing the light of truth to illuminate our path to personal growth, healing, and freedom.

In a world shrouded in falsehoods and half-truths, let us be beacons of honesty, shining forth with unyielding integrity and unwavering resolve. Let us cast aside the chains of deception that bind us, embracing the liberating power of truth-telling with open hearts and steadfast courage. Only when we embrace the truth, however painful it may be, can we break free from the shackles of deceit and step into the fullness of who we were meant to be.

Honesty isn't just a virtue; it's the foundation upon which personal growth thrives. When we strip away the layers of deceit and embrace the unvarnished truth, we create a sacred space for authenticity and vulnerability to flourish. People are drawn to those who wear honesty like a badge of honor, recognizing the integrity and courage it takes to speak the truth even when it's difficult.

Sure, the truth can sting like a fresh wound, but it's also a potent elixir for healing. By bravely confronting our mistakes, flaws, and past traumas, we embark on self-discovery and redemption. Through this process, we unburden ourselves of emotional baggage, finding closure and peace in the unvarnished truth.

Freedom, my friends, is the sweet fruit of living authentically and embracing the truth. When we cast aside the shackles of self-deception and societal expectations, we step into the light of clarity and purpose. The truth becomes our guiding star, leading us toward a life that resonates with our deepest values and beliefs.

The objective truth may be uncomfortable sometimes, but the key lies in personal growth, healing, and freedom. By summoning the courage to confront our truths head-on, we unlock the door to our fullest potential, stepping into a life of authenticity and fulfillment.

So, be bold and brave, and let the truth free you. In its unwavering light lies the power to transform your life in ways you never thought possible. Embrace, cherish, and watch as your world unfolds in beautiful new ways before your very eyes.

Conclusion

In life's journey, we often encounter storms of addiction, toxic relationships, and self-doubt. But through God's unwavering love and guidance, we discover the transformative power of honesty, faith, and self-discovery.

As we peel back the layers of deceit and embrace the unvarnished truth, we create space for authenticity, vulnerability, and personal growth. Through the storms of life, we find strength in our identity as cherished children of God, empowered to lead with courage and conviction.

And though the road may be fraught with challenges and setbacks, we press onward, knowing that with God by our side, we can overcome any obstacle that comes our way. For in His boundless grace and mercy, we find the courage to speak with conviction, the strength to confront our truths, and the freedom to live authentically and purposefully.

So let us be bold, my friends, and let the truth free us. In its unwavering light lies the power to transform our lives in ways we never thought possible. Embrace, cherish, and watch as your world unfolds in beautiful new ways before your very eyes.

5 LET GO AND LET GOD

Sometimes letting things go is an act of far greater power than defending or hanging on.
Life moves on and so should we"
~Spencer Johnson

In the ebb and flow of life, we often cling to things that no longer serve us, be it relationships, jobs, or beliefs. Letting go can be a profound struggle, yet it also holds the key to liberation. As the saying goes, 'Sometimes, releasing is a feat of far greater strength than defending or clinging.' Life propels forward, and so must we. "letting go and letting God" signifies surrendering to a higher power. It involves trusting God to guide our lives and shape our paths. This isn't a sign of weakness; it demonstrates our faith and confidence in His plan.

It's easy to feel overwhelmed and adrift in a world of unpredictability. We often fall into the trap of wanting to micromanage every aspect of our lives, convinced that we know best. But the truth is, we can't always grasp the bigger picture. This is where faith becomes our anchor. We can find solace and purpose amidst the chaos by relinquishing control and allowing God to take the reins.

Surrendering to God's will is crucial. It means releasing our desires and trusting God's plan. Letting go of the illusion of control might be scary, but it opens up endless possibilities. Surrendering to God's will brings true fulfillment and happiness. Impatience often gets the best of us, especially when things don't go as we want. We desire instant gratification and quick results. However, God's timing is perfect. By trusting in His timing, we can find comfort in knowing everything will fall into place at the right time. Trusting in God's timing requires patience and faith, but the rewards are immeasurable.

Growing up in a household rooted in faith, centered on the Gospel, and built on trust and hope, I quickly learned the importance of having a relationship with God. It was more than just a tradition; it was the foundation of my existence. This foundation has shown me that "letting go and letting God" is not just a slogan but a profound way to live a life filled with peace, clarity, and divine purpose. As we release what holds us back in life's journey, we allow God's grace to flow in. And in that divine flow, we discover our true selves, calling, and joy.

My great-grandma, Ms. Elizabeth Kinsey, was a remarkable woman whose faith ran deep. Although I never had the chance to meet her husband, he left an indelible mark on our family. He was a pastor in Panama City, Florida, before the family moved to Syracuse, NY. Long before I was born, the Kinsey family built their foundation on spirituality and the unwavering belief in Yeshua as our Lord and Savior.

My earliest memories are filled with the sound of my nana praying. She prayed daily, and her faith was constantly present in our home. From a young age, my mother and grandma ensured that church was central to my life. Every Sunday, we attended Sunday school and participated in Bible studies. Church wasn't just a place we visited; it was woven into the fabric of our daily lives.

I vividly recall being involved in all the Easter plays, joining the choir, and serving on the usher board. These activities were more than just routines; they taught the importance of fellowship and community. Our family lived by the saying, "A family that prays together stays together." This wasn't just something we said; it was something we lived. My aunts and uncles were all part of the church committee, and our home was filled with worship daily. My family didn't play when it came to faith; they were all in, every day, without fail. It was both serious and full of love and laughter.

However, as I entered my teenage years, I was at a crossroads. The allure of independence and the world beyond the church walls began to tug at my curiosity. I started to question the teachings and values I was raised with, and my focus shifted toward the excitement of worldly things.

During this period, I had a candid conversation with myself and God. I made a bold Declaration, 'Father, I'm ready to take the reins for the next 15-20 years, with you as my silent partner.' I was convinced that I was prepared to navigate life on my terms, according to my desires, not God's. I learned a lot about life and myself. I faced challenges and made mistakes, but through it all, I always felt that gentle nudge, reminding me of the foundation laid for me. Even as I tried to take control, I could feel God's presence, patiently waiting for me to realize that true peace and fulfillment could only come from surrendering to His will.

Looking back, I see those years as a transformative journey of self-discovery and growth. Each step, though at times winding, brought me closer to the faith and values my family had instilled in me. It was a learning process, but every lesson gave me a deeper understanding of the profound meaning of 'letting go and letting God '.

By trying to take control of my own life, I became rebellious, stubborn, and disobedient. This path eventually led me to become a convict, spending many years in and out of county jail until I ended up in state prison. I've had many restless nights running the streets, becoming part of a gang, and starting with marijuana, which escalated to harder drugs like PCP, Molly, and cocaine. Thankfully, I got clean on December 4, 2023.

Not letting God lead my life caused me to drop out of high school, and my dreams of being a student-athlete and a famous rapper vanished. Looking back, I thank God for it, understanding that He had different plans for me. Those long nights in jail and prison, the years of going back and forth to rehab, allowing drugs to control my life, selling myself short, and doing anything for another hit of cocaine led to some of the most embarrassing moments of my life. But through all that, God shaped me into the man I am today.

After years of pain and suffering and finally having a spiritual awakening, I realized that Yeshua had chosen me to do His work. The whole time, I was using my musical talent to degrade women and glorify street life instead of using my voice to spread His message. Now, I understand that God had a greater purpose for me, and it took all those trials to bring me to this realization.

This world is full of hatred, corruption, and evil. Everyone worries about what people think of them and the next trend or topic on social media. It's easy to get distracted and caught up in the chaos. I, too, spent many years being a victim of this, drawn to worldly things instead of paying attention to God's purpose for my life. It took a lot of suffering for me to wake up. I'm not perfect, nor am I super holy. I ask God daily to close my physical eyes and help me see clearly with my spiritual eyes. I ask Him to close my physical ears so I won't miss His whisper and direction with my spiritual ears. I seek

His guidance in all I do now, whereas before, I placed Him last.

Today, I choose to surrender to what I know is best for me, allowing God to lead my life. I had to go through it to grow through it. This journey taught me that every seed needs dirt on its name to blossom.

Surrendering to God doesn't mean giving up or losing control. It means letting go of what weighs us down and trusting in His wisdom and love. When we surrender to God, we open ourselves to His grace and blessings, allowing Him to work miracles in our lives. Surrendering to God's will means aligning our desires with His purpose for our lives. It requires us to let go of our agenda and trust that His plan is far greater than anything we could imagine. By surrendering to God, we can find fulfillment, joy, and peace in His perfect timing.

As the popular song says, "Jesus, take the wheel, take it from my hands." When we allow Jesus to take control of our lives, we can rest assured that He will guide us safely through the storms and challenges that come our way. By taking the backseat and letting Him lead, we can experience His grace and mercy in abundance. I spent years caught up in the wrong crowd. I was rebellious, stubborn, and disobedient, which eventually led me to become a convict. I spent many years in and out of county jail until I ended up in state prison. Those were some of the darkest times of my life. I joined a gang and started using marijuana, which led to harder drugs like PCP, Molly, and cocaine. But on December 4, 2023, I got clean.

Not letting God lead my life caused me to drop out of high school. My dreams of being a student-athlete disappeared, and my aspirations of becoming a famous rapper went down the drain. I thank God for it because He had other plans for me. Those long nights in jail and prison, the years going back and forth to rehab, and allowing drugs to control my life doing anything for another hit of cocaine—led to some of the most embarrassing moments of my life. But through all that, God shaped me into the man I am today.

After years of pain and suffering, I had a spiritual awakening. I realized that I was chosen by Yeshua to do His work. The whole time, I was using my musical talent to degrade women and glorify street life, instead of using my voice to spread His message. Now, I understand that God had a greater purpose for me, and it took all those trials to bring me to this realization.

In times of uncertainty and doubt, seeking God's guidance is important. By turning to Him in prayer and meditation, we can find the clarity and direction we need. God's voice might not always be loud, but if we listen with an open heart, we can trust that He will lead us down the right path. Letting go and letting God is a powerful act of faith. It means giving up our fears, doubts, and insecurities and trusting He will care for us. When we stop trying to control everything and trust in His plan, we feel a sense of freedom and peace beyond understanding.

I've been through a lot of pain and suffering. After years of trying to get clean from drugs letting drugs control my actions and my sexuality deep down, I knew God created man for woman and that my heart yearned for true love between a man and a woman. But during my addiction, I let evil take over. I used my gifts in the wrong way and fed my cocaine habit instead of feeding my spirit. I knew what I was doing was wrong. I wasn't comfortable with it, and I knew the people I was hanging out with were no good for me. I wasn't meant to be part of that crowd. (No disrespect intended; I am just speaking from the heart and what the Gospel says.) Through all those struggles, I learned how important it is to surrender to God. Letting go and letting God take control means allowing Him to work miracles in our lives. We find peace and direction that only He can provide.

Today, I choose to let God lead me. I realize now that all those tough times shaped me into who I am today. When we trust God and let Him guide us, we open ourselves to His grace and blessings. By allowing Jesus take the wheel, we can navigate through the storms and challenges of life, knowing He will lead us safely.

Today, I realize that God had to isolate me. He had to strip away everything I once worshiped: my popularity, ego, and old ways of writing music and rapping about nonsense. He changed my language and showed me how to use my voice to uplift and inspire others by speaking about the gospel.

I used to care so much about fashion and staying fly with all the name brands. I'm happy to keep fresh and clean in a simple sweat suit and New Balance sneakers. I even started my Christian apparel brand. Letting go and letting God humble me completely. I used always to have something to say, or at least I thought I did. Now, I'm slow to speak and quick to listen. I used to be the life of the party, but now I don't even go to parties. Amen. I spent countless hours scrolling on social media and YouTube, following people and pages that added no value to my life. Now, I've deleted some accounts and unfollowed many others, filling my news feed with content that promotes education, spiritual growth, and laughter.

Looking back, I have lost many things I wanted to hold onto so badly, but today, those things hold no value. I admit I've done things that may have pushed away people I thought were friends. But now I realize no true friend will abandon you at your low points. God was removing people who meant no good to me before the good in me came to life.

When we let go and let God guide our steps, we allow Him to lead us down the path He has planned for us. This requires faith and trust in His wisdom. We can avoid unnecessary detours and pitfalls by listening to His voice and following His direction. Letting God guide us ensures we are on the right path towards our destiny.

Now, I choose to let God lead me. All those tough times shaped me into who I am now. By allowing Jesus to take the wheel, we can navigate through the storms and challenges of life, knowing He will lead us safely.

In life, we face tough times that test our strength. Sometimes, people come and go, which can feel like a loss. But looking back, I see that God was removing people who weren't good for me before the good in me could shine through.

Through my pain, I discovered the beauty of letting go and letting God work in mysterious ways to bring positivity and growth into our lives. In tough times, it's hard to see the bigger picture. But God often sends signs to show us who should stay and who should go. It could be conflicts, misunderstandings, or a feeling in our gut. Feeling hurt when people leave is normal, especially if we care about them. But true healing comes from being grateful for the lessons and trusting that God has a plan for us. We can move forward with peace when we let go of bitterness and trust in God.

Getting rid of negative influences is like a miracle. It makes room for good things to come into our lives. By embracing this miracle and leaving the past behind, we can create a brighter future filled with love and joy. Letting go and letting God is a spiritual journey. It takes faith, patience, and a strong connection to our higher power. We can transform our lives in amazing ways when we surrender control and let God lead us.

Trusting in God's plan is important as we experience life's ups and downs. Even if we don't understand why certain people leave, we can believe that it's for our good. By accepting what comes our way, we can find peace amid chaos. Letting go and letting God work in our lives is a beautiful experience. By recognizing signs, being grateful, embracing miracles, starting a spiritual journey, and seeking understanding, we can face life's challenges with strength and grace.

Trusting in God's plan is like navigating through a dense fog. We can't always see what lies ahead, but we have faith that God knows the way even when we can't see it ourselves. Looking back on my journey, I'm grateful for the people God removed from my life. It might have felt like a loss at the time, but now I see it as a necessary step for the good within me to shine through.

Letting go and letting God isn't just a simple act; it's a profound spiritual journey. It's about surrendering our desires, fears, and worries to God's care. It's about acknowledging that God's plan for us is far greater than anything we could imagine. And it's about trusting that He will guide us to where we need to be, even if the path is unclear.

For those who haven't experienced this surrender yet, I want you to know that it's not about giving up control; it's about gaining freedom. It's about releasing our burdens and allowing God to carry them. It's about recognizing that we are not alone in this journey and that God is always with us, ready to guide us if we're willing to listen.

Surrendering our will to God is a powerful concept that can bring about profound changes in our lives. It's about letting go of the past, the mistakes, regrets, and hurts, and embracing the future with hope and anticipation. It's about forgiving ourselves and others so that we can move forward unencumbered by the weight of the past.

The past is something we cannot change, no matter how much we might wish we could. Holding onto it only anchors us in place, preventing us from moving forward. But by letting go, forgiving, and trusting in God's plan, we can break free from the chains of the past and step into the future with confidence and joy.

When we talk about surrendering to God, we hand over the steering wheel of our lives and trust Him to navigate us toward a bright and promising future. It's not always easy, especially when we're used to being in control, but it's a powerful act of faith that can lead to incredible transformations.

To create a better future, we've got to be willing to make changes in our lives. Sometimes, that means letting go of things holding us back, habits that drag us down, relationships that drain our energy, or beliefs that limit our potential. It's not always comfortable, but when we surrender to God's guidance, He helps us shed what no longer serves us and opens the door to new possibilities.

The past can be tricky. It's like a ghost that haunts our present, whispering regrets and what-ifs in our ears. But the truth is, dwelling on the past only robs us of the joy and potential of the present moment. Surrendering to God means letting go of those old hurts and mistakes, forgiving ourselves and others, and embracing the life waiting for us.

But surrendering to God isn't a one-and-done kind of deal. It's a daily practice. It's about inviting God into every aspect of our lives, big and small, and trusting Him to guide us in the right direction. It's about seeking His wisdom in every decision we make and finding peace in knowing that His plan is always better than anything we could come up with.

When we surrender to God in this way, something incredible happens. We start to see our lives transformed from the inside out. We find purpose where there was confusion, joy where there was sorrow, and love where there was fear. It's a journey filled with ups and downs, twists and turns, but through it all, we're held in God's hand, safe and secure in His love.

So, if you're feeling lost or overwhelmed, remember that you don't have to go alone. Trust in God, surrender to His will and watch as He transforms your life in ways you never thought possible. It's a journey that leads to a future filled with hope, purpose, and fulfillment.

Letting go and letting God take control means giving Him the power to shape our future. It's about trusting His plan, even when we can't see where it's going. When we stop trying to control everything and let God lead, we can finally relax and find real peace. Trusting in God and surrendering to His will isn't always easy, but it's incredibly rewarding. When we let go of what we think we want and let God guide us, we discover a deeper sense of purpose and fulfillment.
It's like finally finding the right path after wandering lost for so long.

From my own life, I know that letting go and letting God can change everything. It's about putting down the heavy burdens we've been carrying and letting God take over. When we trust Him, we find peace, purpose, and joy that we never knew before. It takes faith to trust God's plan, especially when life is tough. But when we stop worrying and let God handle our problems, we open ourselves up to His guidance. It's like lifting a huge weight off our shoulders and letting God show us the way.

Letting go isn't weak; it's actually very strong. It takes real courage to stop trying to control everything and believe that God has a better plan for us. When we do this, we find new possibilities and a better future waiting for us.

Surrendering to God means trusting that He knows what's best, even when we don't understand it. It's about letting go of our fears and letting God work His miracles in our lives. So, let go of what's holding you back, and let God lead you to a life filled with hope, purpose, and happiness.

CONCLUSION

Dear reader! Always remember one thing: the power and peace found in letting go and letting God take control. Life often throws us challenges and obstacles that can shake our faith. It's during these tough times that trusting in God becomes most important. When we surrender our struggles to Him and trust in His divine plan, we find the strength and peace to overcome anything.

Stress and anxiety often come from trying to control everything ourselves. By letting go and allowing God to guide us, we can release the burden of worry and find true peace. Surrendering to God's will means letting go of what weighs us down and finding freedom in His grace.

Trying to handle everything on our own can lead to feeling overwhelmed and burnt out. But when we surrender to God and let Him take over, we find rest and peace in His presence. Trusting in God's perfect timing and provision allows us to let go of our need to control every outcome.

Life is a journey full of ups and downs. In moments of uncertainty, we must remember to let go and let God. By trusting in His plan, we can find the peace and strength to face any challenge. Letting go is an act of faith and courage, and it holds far greater power than clinging to control. Trust in God, have faith that He will provide, and allow Him to work in your life. Let go, trust in God, and watch as He leads you to a life filled with peace, joy, and purpose.

6 LETTING GO OF THE PAST

Holding on is believing that there's only a past; letting go is knowing there's a future."
~Daphne Rose Kingma

Letting Go: Embracing the Future

Letting go is often easier said than done. It requires deepseated courage and a willingness to confront the past, acknowledge its influence, and ultimately release its hold on our lives. Yet, within this act lies the promise of renewal, of embracing a future filled with hope, possibility, and purpose.

At the heart of letting go is recognizing the power of the past. Our past experiences, both positive and negative, shape our perceptions, beliefs, and behaviors. They weave a narrative that informs our present reality and influences our future trajectory. But clinging too tightly to the past can become a burden, weighing us down with regret, resentment, or fear. It can hinder our ability to grow, evolve, and fully engage with the opportunities that lie ahead.

There are no dreams in Letting Go of What I Am Not; it is more about acknowledging the absence of the past. It is about setting a limit and reconciling with its existence without becoming a prisoner of its hold over us. It means understanding that one's past is part of one's story up to the present, but one's future does not have to be only the same. Letting go means we stop clinging to that which hinders transformation for a brighter tomorrow and a new perception of life.

Embracing the future requires a leap of faith and a willingness to step into the unknown with courage and conviction. It means trusting in ourselves, in our resilience, and in our capacity to navigate the challenges that lie ahead. It means believing we have the strength and the resources to overcome obstacles and create a life filled with meaning and purpose.

Forgiving – when it comes to maintaining it – is a process, a special and unique path of a man whose goal is to discover himself and become reborn. Change is the biggest challenge that can be handled only when one is patient and willing to face discomfort when making a change and showing compassion. It could imply having to release a particular way of being, a certain type of connection, or passion that once was meaningful but now reeks of stagnancy. A band, however, releases another album with the prospect of evolving, developing, progressing, and progressing to the next level.

Letting go is also an act of liberation. It frees us from the shackles of the past, the burdens of regret or resentment, and the limitations of our self-imposed barriers. It allows us to reclaim our agency, take ownership of our lives, and chart a course aligned with our deepest values and aspirations.

Embracing the future is an act of faith. It's about trusting that the universe has a plan for us, that there is a purpose to our journey, and that each step forward brings us closer to our truest selves. It's about recognizing that every ending is also a beginning, every setback is an opportunity for growth, and every challenge is a chance to shine.

It is the freedom to come to terms with life in its entirety, to accept life with all its ups and downs, and to die with dignity. It conveys that one does not have to and should not be confined or bound by the decisions one has made before but that one needs to look forward and have a good outlook on what is to come. Therefore, let's let go, dear reader, and with compelled force, allow yourself to capture a glimpse of hope as you move forward.

Acknowledging the Power of the Past

The past has an undeniable influence on our lives. It shapes our beliefs, molds our perceptions, and subtly and profoundly influences our actions. From childhood experiences to formative relationships, our past is a tapestry woven with memories, emotions, and lessons learned.

Acknowledging the power of the past is the first step towards understanding its impact on our present reality. It's about recognizing how past experiences have shaped our beliefs about ourselves, others, and the world. Whether positive or negative, these experiences imprint on our psyche, influencing our thoughts, behaviors, and attitudes in the present.

For many, the past can provide comfort, providing a sense of identity and continuity in an ever-changing world. Fond memories of childhood adventures, family gatherings, or personal achievements anchor the sea of life's uncertainties. These cherished moments remind us of who we are, where we come from, and the values that guide us.

But the past can also be negative, reminding us of the memories of past failures, pain, or simply regrets. September marks a time when people often think about hopes and opportunities; it is a great time to remind ourselves about unresolved conflicts, broken relationships, and missed opportunities that can affect our happiness now and dreams in the future. Sometimes, we are in a position where past failures and our failures, in general, may prevent us from going further, as they constantly put us behind by sowing the seeds of doubt and fear within us.

Yet, in acknowledging the power of the past, we also recognize its potential for growth and transformation. Every experience, whether positive or negative, offers an opportunity for learning and personal development. Mistakes teach us valuable lessons, failures build resilience, and setbacks foster perseverance. By embracing the lessons of the past, we can cultivate wisdom, empathy, and strength that enrich our lives and deepen our understanding of ourselves and others.

Recognizing the potential of forgetting the past demonstrates the ability to take charge of our lives. Though where we are from is unchangeable, the way we are now and the events we can influence are open. We can apologize for errors while not being imprisoned by them, grant pardons to offenders while not patronizing their misconduct, and move on from injuries while not erasing their consequences. In this way, we let go of feelings such as resentment, regret, or bitterness, which helps to overcome these negative outcomes.

Admitting the role of the past is also an appeal to being present and helping others be aware of themselves. We can wonder about our past experiences and get to know them, making us aware of patterns in our behaviors and thoughts and what we believe in. We become aware of such things as hidden prejudices, personal assumptions, and developing destructive patterns of habits that might hinder our progress. With this understanding, we can deliberately disembowel ourselves from clinging to dangerous things and nurture positive psychology and hope instead.

When we acknowledge the power of the past, we recognize its role as a teacher. Every experience, whether joyful or painful, carries valuable lessons if we're willing to listen. Reflecting on past successes can reinforce our strengths and abilities, while examining past mistakes can reveal areas for growth and improvement. By embracing these lessons, we empower ourselves to make more informed choices and navigate future challenges with greater wisdom and resilience.

However, there is some truth to the idea that remembering something is also a way of respecting it; it is a way of remembering our history. It's about understanding how today became possible – the choices made and the doors opened, the paths veered from, and the obstacles surmounted. It's been enlightening to realize that every experience has taken part in building the person we are now, with its advantages and fears, dreams and weaknesses. Man thus affirms his being and his station in the universe by accepting and accepting his history and endowing himself with a positive message or principle of existence.

Still, understanding history's strength includes facing certain truths about what it entails. Trauma, loss, or betrayal that occurred in the past is not easy to forget; on the contrary, one may feel it is always present with them as if it casts a shadow on them. They may have had some devastating effects on us- mentally, emotionally, and physically. Yet, it is only by exposing these unknown injuries, by simply recognizing them as existing, that we begin the process of the wounded's healing and deliverance. It is through counseling, taking care of oneself, or speaking to friends and family that the hold of the past is let go of, and its negative impact on one's well-being is minimized.

Furthermore, acknowledging the power of the past invites us to explore the intergenerational legacy that shapes our lives. Our family history, cultural heritage, and societal influences all contribute to the lens through which we view the world. By examining these inherited narratives with curiosity and compassion, we gain insight into the patterns and beliefs limiting us. We can then honor the parts of our heritage that resonate with our values and identity while letting go of those that no longer serve us.

In essence, acknowledging the power of the past is a dynamic and ongoing process. It's about embracing the complexity of our experiences, light and shadow, and finding meaning and growth in every moment. It's about recognizing that our past does not define us but informs our journey toward self-discovery and self-actualization. By honoring the lessons, the journey, and ourselves, we open ourselves to a future filled with possibility, authenticity, and joy.

The Courage to Move Forward

The Courage to Move Forward is a testament to the human spirit's resilience in adversity and uncertainty. It embodies the willingness to confront challenges, embrace change, and pursue new opportunities, even when the path ahead is unclear or daunting. At its core, the courage to move forward is not merely about overcoming fear but about summoning the strength and determination to take decisive action to pursue our goals and aspirations.

One crucial aspect of the courage to move forward is confronting and overcoming fear. Fear often holds us back from taking risks and seizing opportunities, trapping us in our comfort zones and preventing us from realizing our full potential. However, by acknowledging our fears and facing them head-on, we can diminish their power over us and liberate ourselves to pursue our dreams with courage and conviction.

However, one must proceed forward—and for the latter, resistance involves tenacity, the ability to overcome obstacles, and power through. As we go through life, many hurdles, barriers, and stumbling blocks can pose threats and hinder us. But that is where the culture of resilience comes in; it means that we can face the highs and lows of life and emerge a more resilient version of ourselves on the other side.

The second component of courage, or the ability to move on, is the willingness to change and positively use the force of habit. Transition is a part of life and cannot be avoided: one must leap forward and put oneself in the line when the sun rises again. As the phrase implies, change may be seen as scary and negative, but it can also be used to develop, excel, and find oneself. These tips show that with an open mind and a positive attitude, people can welcome change and face it with the best attitude possible to improve on their new circumstances.

Besides, fear is overcome by facing it, letting go of what no longer matters, and embracing change actively. It is important to let go of things, individuals, or situations that keep one stuck in the past but unable to gain ground. On the other hand, as people embrace surrender, it means to let go of those energies draining us. They open the door for new energies and possibilities in one's life, thus opening new cycles of change.

Ultimately, the courage to move forward is a choice – a decision to take control of our destiny and create the life we desire. It is about stepping out of our comfort zones, embracing uncertainty, and passionately pursuing our dreams. While the journey forward may be fraught with challenges and obstacles, it is also filled with boundless potential and opportunities for growth and fulfillment.

Moving forward requires courage, resilience, and a willingness to embrace change. It involves confronting our fears, overcoming setbacks, and staying committed to our goals, even when the going gets tough. By summoning the courage to move forward, we empower ourselves to transcend limitations, unlock our full potential, and create a life of purpose, passion, and meaning.

Besides, the desire and willingness to act and change imply the need for help and advice, especially when the going gets tough. Whether it is companionship, reliance on those closest to us during a difficult time, or even guidance from individuals with more wisdom and experience, it is easier to face life with more tenacity and assurance when we have a healthy social support system.

In conclusion, the courage to move forward is a powerful force that propels us toward our goals and aspirations, even in the face of uncertainty and adversity. It is a testament to the indomitable human spirit and our capacity to overcome challenges and setbacks. By embracing change, confronting our fears, and staying true to our dreams, we can move forward with confidence and conviction, knowing that the path ahead is filled with endless possibilities for growth and fulfillment.

Creating Space for New Beginnings

Creating space for new beginnings is a multifaceted process encompassing various dimensions of our lives, touching upon internal and external aspects of our existence. As we explore this transformative journey, it becomes evident that there are several key components to consider, each contributing to our ability to embrace change and transition with openness and resilience.

Forgiveness emerges as a fundamental aspect of creating space for new beginnings. By releasing ourselves from the burdens of past resentments and grievances, we open up space in our hearts and minds for healing and growth. Forgiveness allows us to let go of old wounds and make room for new connections and experiences to enter our lives, fostering a sense of liberation and renewal.

Accepting paradoxes and mysteries when dealing with the intricacies of life's changes is crucial. When we recognize the natural uncertainties and conflicts that come with change, we develop humility and curiosity, which enables us to accept uncertainty with elegance and strength. Embracing paradoxes encourages us to investigate life's enigmas with an open attitude, accepting the unfamiliar as a vital component of the path toward fresh starts.

Forging space for new beginnings demands us to foster surrender and trust in life's journey, alongside forgiveness and acceptance of paradox. Letting go of the need for control and certainty enables us to release resistance and greet the present moment with openness and embrace. Embracing the inherent wisdom of the universe, even in uncertain times, empowers us to welcome new opportunities and experiences with faith and hope.

Taking care of ourselves and nurturing our well-being is crucial for supporting us through periods of change. Giving importance to activities that nourish our physical, mental, and spiritual health enables us to renew our energy and build resilience. Participating in physical exercise, mindfulness, and immersing ourselves in nature promotes a feeling of inner tranquility and equilibrium, giving us the strength to navigate life's changes more smoothly and gracefully.

Gratitude emerges as another essential aspect of creating space for new beginnings. By cultivating gratitude, we shift our focus from scarcity to abundance, recognizing the blessings surrounding us every moment. Practicing gratitude allows us to find joy and fulfillment in the present, even amidst life's challenges and uncertainties, fostering a sense of appreciation for the richness of life's experiences.

Setting intentions and using visualization are effective tools for achieving our dreams and ambitions. When we establish clear intentions for what we want to achieve, we focus our energy on our desired results. Visualization lets us mentally practice our objectives, making them seem more real and achievable. When we align our thoughts, beliefs, and actions with our intentions, we can take motivated steps toward realizing our dreams, paving the way for new opportunities to emerge.

Creating space for new beginnings is a holistic and transformative journey that requires courage, openness, and resilience. By embracing forgiveness, paradox, surrender, self-care, gratitude, intention setting, and visualization, we create a fertile ground for new opportunities and experiences to flourish. As we navigate life's transitions, may we approach the journey of making space for new beginnings with authenticity, curiosity, and an open heart, trusting in the wisdom of the universe to guide us toward a future filled with growth, joy, and abundance

Learning from Setbacks

Learning from setbacks is integral to the human experience, profoundly shaping our growth and resilience. Setbacks, whether they are failures, disappointments, or challenges, offer invaluable lessons that can propel us forward on our journey toward personal and professional development.

At its core, learning from setbacks requires a mindset shift. Instead of viewing setbacks as obstacles to be avoided or ignored, we can see them as opportunities for growth and learning. By reframing setbacks as valuable learning experiences, we empower ourselves to extract meaningful lessons from even the most difficult situations.

One key aspect of learning from setbacks is embracing failure as a natural and inevitable part of the process. Failure is not a reflection of our worth or abilities but rather a stepping stone towards success. By embracing failure with humility and curiosity, we can uncover valuable insights into our strengths, weaknesses, and areas for improvement.

Learning from setbacks enables us to bounce back from adversity with strength and determination. Resilience is not about avoiding setbacks but developing the inner resources to withstand and overcome them. By building resilience, we become better equipped to navigate life's challenges and setbacks gracefully and confidently.

Let's talk about seeking feedback and support from others; it can happen by learning from setbacks. It's about reaching out to mentors, colleagues, or friends for guidance and perspective and being open to constructive criticism. By seeking feedback, we gain valuable insights into our blind spots and areas for growth, allowing us to course-correct and move forward with greater clarity and confidence.

Ultimately, learning from setbacks is a continuous process of growth and self-improvement. It requires us to embrace failure as a natural part of the learning journey, cultivate resilience in the face of adversity, engage in reflection and self-assessment, and seek feedback and support from others. By approaching setbacks with a growth mindset and a willingness to learn, we can turn even the most challenging experiences into opportunities for growth and development.

Living with Purpose and Integrity

Living with purpose and integrity is a profound journey that encompasses various aspects of the human experience, requiring continuous self-reflection, growth, and commitment. At its core, it's about aligning our actions with our values and beliefs, striving to impact the world around us positively, and living authentically, even in the face of challenges or obstacles.

One essential aspect of living with purpose and integrity is cultivating resilience in the face of adversity. Life is filled with challenges and setbacks that can test our resolve and shake our sense of purpose. However, we can weather life's storms with grace and determination by developing resilience and emerging stronger and more resilient than before. Resilience is not about avoiding difficulties or denying their impact; rather, it's about our ability to bounce back from setbacks and adversity, learning and growing from these experiences. When we face challenges with resilience, we demonstrate our commitment to living with integrity, refusing to be defeated by life's obstacles.

Yes, it involves embracing vulnerability as a source of strength rather than weakness. However, It's about allowing ourselves to be seen and heard authentically, without pretense or armor. By embracing vulnerability, we foster deeper connections with others and create space for genuine relationships built on trust and authenticity.

Living with purpose and integrity also requires cultivating empathy and compassion for others. It's about recognizing the humanity in each individual and extending kindness and understanding to those around us. Practicing empathy fosters a sense of interconnectedness and belonging, contributing to a more compassionate and inclusive world.

Our values and beliefs align with it, even when challenging or inconvenient. It's about living with integrity in our personal and professional lives, honoring our commitments and responsibilities with honesty and authenticity. However, living with purpose and integrity also entails embracing growth and learning as lifelong processes.

It's about approaching life with a growth mindset, viewing challenges as personal and professional development opportunities. By embracing continuous learning and growth, we expand our horizons, deepen our understanding of ourselves and the world around us, and cultivate resilience and adaptability in the face of change.

Ultimately, living with purpose and integrity is a dynamic and ongoing journey that requires dedication, courage, and commitment. It's about striving to be the best version of ourselves, living in alignment with our values and beliefs, and positively impacting the world.

As we navigate the complexities of life, we may encounter moments of doubt, uncertainty, and fear. However, during these challenging times, our commitment to living with purpose and integrity is put to the test. We must draw upon our inner strength and resilience during these moments, reaffirm our values and beliefs, and recommit ourselves to our journey.

One thing to remember is that living with purpose and integrity can be challenging but deeply rewarding. It's about living a life of meaning and significance, guided by our deepest values and aspirations. It's about making a difference in the lives of others and leaving a positive legacy for future generations.

In short, living with purpose and integrity is a journey of self-discovery, growth, and transformation. It's about embracing our vulnerabilities, cultivating resilience, and making conscious choices that align with our values and beliefs. By living with purpose and integrity, we can create a life of authenticity, meaning, and fulfillment, leaving a lasting impact on the world around us.

Choosing Self-Improvement

Choosing self-improvement is a transformative journey encompassing various dimensions of our lives, from physical well-being to emotional and spiritual growth. At its core, it reflects a commitment to personal growth and development, involving a conscious effort to enhance various aspects of oneself. By choosing self-improvement, individuals embark on self-discovery, self-awareness, and continuous learning, striving to become their best versions.

One crucial aspect of choosing self-improvement is cultivating resilience and perseverance. Life presents numerous challenges and setbacks that can test our resolve and confidence. However, by developing resilience, we can bounce back from adversity stronger and more resilient than before. Resilience is not about avoiding difficulties but rather about our ability to adapt and grow in the face of adversity. By cultivating resilience, we navigate life's challenges with greater ease and grace, becoming more empowered.

Why choose self-improvement? The answer is simple and clear. It involves cultivating self-compassion and acceptance. It's about treating ourselves with kindness, understanding, and forgiveness, especially during struggle or failure. Self-compassion allows us to gracefully embrace our imperfections and shortcomings, recognizing our inherent worthiness. By cultivating self-compassion, we foster a deeper sense of self-worth and inner peace, empowering us to thrive in all areas of our lives.

Further, choosing self-improvement requires a commitment to holistic well-being. This involves nurturing physical, mental, emotional, and spiritual health through regular self-care practices. Prioritizing self-care enables us to maintain balance and harmony, replenishing our energy and reducing stress. By enhancing our overall well-being, we show up as our best selves in all aspects of life.

Does self-improvement involve cultivating healthy habits and routines? Yes, because it supports our goals and aspirations. Whether adopting a nutritious diet, getting enough sleep, or practicing stress management techniques, healthy habits lay the foundation for personal growth. By making conscious choices and prioritizing our health and well-being, we create a solid framework for self-improvement.

Let's talk about a growth mindset. Choosing self-improvement necessitates embracing a growth mindset-believing that our abilities and intelligence can be developed through dedication and effort. People with a growth mindset view challenges as opportunities for growth rather than obstacles to be avoided. They embrace setbacks as learning opportunities and persist in the face of adversity, knowing they can achieve their goals with time and effort.

Self-improvement requires stepping out of our comfort zone and embracing new experiences. Growth often occurs outside our comfort zones, where we stretch our limits and expand our capabilities. By embracing discomfort and uncertainty, we open ourselves to new opportunities for learning and growth, becoming more resilient and adaptable.

The journey of self-discovery, empowerment, and fulfillment is simply self-improvement. It involves recognizing our potential for growth and taking proactive steps toward becoming the best version of ourselves. By embracing resilience, self-compassion, holistic well-being, healthy habits, a growth mindset, and stepping out of our comfort zones, we unlock our full potential and create a life of purpose, passion, and meaning.

Being Mindful of Others

Being mindful of others is essential to fostering meaningful connections, cultivating empathy, and nurturing harmonious relationships in personal and professional settings. It involves developing an awareness of the thoughts, feelings, and needs of those around us and showing compassion, kindness, and respect in our interactions. Practicing mindfulness toward others can create a supportive and inclusive environment where everyone feels valued, understood, and appreciated.

At its core, being mindful of others requires us to be fully present in our interactions and attentive to the cues and signals conveyed by those around us. This means listening actively, without judgment or distraction, and offering our full attention to the person speaking. By being present and engaged in our interactions, we signal to others that we value and respect their perspectives, fostering mutual trust and understanding.

The ability to understand and share another person's feelings is simply being mindful of others. Empathy allows us to connect with others more deeply, recognizing their emotions and experiences as valid and worthy of acknowledgment. By empathizing with others, we demonstrate compassion and support, validating their feelings and offering comfort and understanding in times of need.

In addition to empathy, being mindful of others requires us to practice kindness and compassion in our interactions. Kindness involves generosity, warmth, and goodwill towards others, while compassion entails showing concern and care for their well-being. By practicing kindness and compassion, we create a positive and uplifting atmosphere where everyone feels valued and supported, enhancing the quality of our relationships and fostering a sense of belonging and connection.

Being mindful of others involves respecting their boundaries, preferences, and autonomy. It's essential to recognize that each person has unique perspectives, needs, and boundaries and honor these differences with sensitivity and understanding. By respecting others' boundaries and autonomy, we demonstrate integrity and empathy, fostering trust and mutual respect in our relationships.

It entails recognizing the impact of our words and actions on those around us. However, It's essential to consider how our behavior may affect others and to take responsibility for our actions, apologizing and making amends when necessary. By being mindful of the consequences of our behavior, we can cultivate empathy and compassion in our interactions, fostering a culture of kindness and respect.

It also involves actively seeking opportunities to support and uplift those in need. This may include offering a listening ear, providing practical assistance, or simply being present for someone struggling. By helping others, we demonstrate empathy and compassion, creating a supportive and nurturing environment where everyone feels valued and supported.

Let's talk about the factor of supporting others. Being mindful also involves recognizing and appreciating the contributions of those around us. It's essential to express gratitude and acknowledgment for the efforts and achievements of others, recognizing their contributions and celebrating their successes. By showing appreciation for others, we cultivate a culture of positivity and encouragement, fostering a sense of camaraderie and teamwork in our interactions.

It requires us to be open-minded and receptive to feedback and constructive criticism. However, It's essential to approach interactions with humility and a willingness to learn from others, recognizing that everyone has valuable insights and perspectives. By being open to feedback, we can cultivate a growth mindset and continue to learn and grow personally and professionally.

Ultimately, being mindful of others is about fostering a culture of empathy, kindness, and respect in our interactions. It's about recognizing the humanity in others and treating them with compassion, dignity, and understanding. By practicing mindfulness towards others, we can create a supportive and inclusive environment where everyone feels valued, respected, and appreciated, enriching our relationships and enhancing the quality of our lives.

Trusting in God's Guidance

The only benefit we gain from the past is the experiences we can learn from, grow wiser, move forward, and use that experience to bring you and another human being closer to God.

~Rondell Kinsey Jr

Trusting in God's guidance is a profound expression of faith and surrender to a higher power's wisdom and providence. It involves relinquishing control and trusting divine guidance to navigate life's challenges and uncertainties. This trust is rooted in the belief that God has a plan for each individual's life and that everything happens for a purpose, even if the reasons are not immediately apparent.

At its core, trusting in God's guidance requires a deep sense of surrender and humility. It involves acknowledging one's limitations and recognizing higher forces at work beyond human comprehension. By surrendering to God's will, individuals open themselves to divine intervention and guidance, allowing them to find peace and clarity amidst life's trials and tribulations.

God's guidance involves cultivating a relationship with the divine through prayer, meditation, and spiritual practices.

These practices help individuals connect with God's presence and discern His will for their lives. By quieting the mind and opening the heart to divine guidance, individuals can receive insights, inspiration, and direction to guide them on their spiritual journey.

The additional factors of prayer, meditation, and trusting God's guidance require patience and perseverance. Divine timing may not always align with human expectations, and answers to prayers may not come immediately. However, by remaining steadfast in faith and trust, individuals can rest assured that God's timing is perfect and that He works all things together for good.

What is involved in God's guidance? Trusting in God's guidance consists of letting go of fear and doubt and embracing a mindset of faith and confidence. It's about releasing worries about the future and trusting that God's plan is unfolding exactly as it should. By surrendering to God's guidance, individuals can find peace and serenity, knowing that a loving and compassionate higher power is guiding them.

Let God control and work in mysterious ways. It's about releasing attachments to specific outcomes and trusting that God's plan is always for the highest good, even if it may not align with one's desires or expectations. By surrendering to God's will, individuals can experience freedom and peace, knowing they align with divine purpose and guidance.

To surrender and align, trusting in God's guidance requires discernment and discerning God's voice amidst the noise and distractions of the world. It's about cultivating a deep connection with God through prayer, meditation, and spiritual practices and learning to recognize His voice and guidance in one's heart and intuition. By honing the ability to discern God's guidance, individuals can navigate life's challenges with greater clarity and confidence, knowing they are led by divine wisdom and insight.

Trusting in God's guidance is a profound journey that unfolds over time, requiring continuous faith, surrender, and alignment with divine will. As individuals deepen their trust in God's guidance, they may encounter various challenges and tests of faith that ultimately strengthen their spiritual resolve and deepen their connection with the divine.

One crucial aspect of trusting in God's guidance is maintaining faith during times of uncertainty and adversity. Life is full of unexpected twists and turns, and individuals may face trials and tribulations that test their faith and trust in God's plan. However, by leaning on their faith and trusting in God's unwavering love and providence, individuals can find solace and strength amidst life's storms, knowing they are never alone and God is always guiding them toward their highest good.

God's guidance requires patience and perseverance. Divine timing may not always align with human expectations, and answers to prayers may not come immediately. However, by remaining steadfast in faith and trust, individuals can rest assured that God's timing is perfect and that He works all things together for good. By patiently awaiting God's guidance and remaining open to His divine intervention, individuals can navigate life's challenges with grace and resilience, knowing a loving and compassionate higher power guides them. Recognizing and embracing God's presence is important. It's about cultivating a deep awareness of God's love and guidance, even amid life's challenges and uncertainties. By practicing mindfulness and staying attuned to God's presence, individuals can experience a profound sense of peace and security, knowing they are always held in the loving embrace of divine grace.

Are humans fallible and limited in understanding God's wisdom? Trusting in God's guidance involves embracing humility and acknowledging dependence on the divine. It's about recognizing that humans are fallible and limited in understanding while God's wisdom and providence are infinite and all-encompassing. By humbly surrendering to God's guidance, individuals can experience a profound sense of liberation and empowerment, knowing they are guided by a higher power's divine wisdom and insight.

Ultimately, trusting in God's guidance is a transformative journey that requires faith, surrender, and alignment with divine will. It's about acknowledging God as the ultimate source of wisdom and guidance and seeking His will in all aspects of life. By surrendering control, aligning with divine purpose, practicing patience and perseverance, and embracing humility and mindfulness, individuals can experience the peace, fulfillment, and abundance that come from trusting in God's perfect plan.

Taking Action for Change

Taking action for change is a proactive and empowering approach to creating positive transformations in various aspects of life, from personal growth to social justice advocacy. It involves recognizing the need for change, setting clear goals, and taking decisive steps to achieve the desired outcomes. Whether addressing individual challenges or larger societal issues, taking action for change requires courage, determination, and a commitment to making a difference.

At its core, taking action for change begins with awareness and recognizing the need for improvement or progress. It involves acknowledging areas of concern or injustice and refusing to accept the status quo. Individuals can lay the groundwork for meaningful change by focusing on issues requiring attention and inspiring others to join their efforts.

Action for change requires setting clear and achievable goals that align with one's values and aspirations. Whether seeking personal growth or advocating for social justice, setting specific objectives provides a roadmap for action and helps maintain focus and momentum. Individuals can measure their progress by defining tangible outcomes and adjusting their strategies to stay on course toward their goals.

Setting goals and taking action for change involves planning and implementing strategies to achieve those goals effectively. This may include conducting research, building coalitions, mobilizing resources, and leveraging various platforms and channels to raise awareness and drive engagement. Individuals can maximize their impact by developing comprehensive action plans and creating sustainable change over time.

It requires courage and resilience in the face of obstacles and opposition. Change is often met with resistance from internal doubts and fears or external barriers and naysayers. However, by summoning the courage to persevere in adversity, individuals can overcome obstacles and stay committed to their goals, knowing their efforts make a difference.

Collaboration and collective action, recognizing that meaningful change often requires the efforts of many working together toward a common purpose. By building alliances, sharing resources, and amplifying each other's voices, individuals can leverage collective power to effect change on a larger scale. Collaboration fosters synergy, creativity, and resilience, enabling individuals and communities to achieve more together than they could alone.

Action for change requires an ongoing commitment to learning and growth, recognizing that change is dynamic and iterative. It's essential to remain open-minded, adaptable, and receptive to feedback, continually refining strategies and approaches based on new information and insights. By embracing a growth mindset, individuals can overcome challenges more effectively and evolve tactics to drive meaningful, sustainable change.

It is about making a difference and positively impacting the world around us. Whether advocating for social justice, promoting environmental sustainability, or pursuing personal development, every action can create ripple effects and inspire others to join the movement for change. By leading by example and embodying the values of courage, determination, and compassion, individuals can contribute to a brighter and more equitable future for all.

It includes recognizing and addressing systemic barriers and injustices perpetuating inequality and oppression. It's about advocating for policies and practices that promote fairness, inclusivity, and social justice and challenging systems of power and privilege that perpetuate discrimination and marginalization. By speaking out against injustice and working to dismantle oppressive structures, individuals can create a more just and equitable society for future generations.

Yes, it requires empathy and compassion for those impacted by injustice and inequality. It's essential to listen to and uplift the voices of marginalized communities, centering their experiences and perspectives in the fight for social change. By solidarity with those most affected by injustice, individuals can amplify their voices and advocate for meaningful solutions that address root causes and create lasting change.

Advocacy and activism involve initiating change by fostering dialogue and promoting understanding across diverse perspectives and experiences. It's about creating spaces for constructive conversations and mutual respect, where differences are celebrated and common ground is sought. Individuals can bridge divides and build coalitions that advance shared goals and values by engaging in respectful dialogue and seeking common solutions.

Living in the Present Moment

Living in the present moment is a practice that invites individuals to fully engage with their immediate experiences, free from the distractions of the past or the anxieties about the future. It involves cultivating mindfulness and awareness of the here and now, appreciating each moment as it unfolds with openness, curiosity, and acceptance. By anchoring oneself in the present moment, individuals can experience greater clarity, peace, and fulfillment.

At its core, living in the present moment requires letting go of regrets and resentments from the past and releasing worries and anxieties about the future. It's about recognizing that the only moment we have is the present and making the most of it. By freeing ourselves from the burdens of the past and the uncertainties of the future, we can experience a profound sense of liberation and empowerment, fully embracing the richness and beauty of life in the here and now.

It focuses on our thoughts, feelings, and sensations without judgment or attachment. Mindfulness allows us to become more aware of our inner experiences and external surroundings, enabling us to respond to life's challenges with greater clarity and stability. By training our minds to be present and focused, we can cultivate a deeper sense of inner peace and resilience in the face of stress and adversity.

This moment requires practicing gratitude and appreciation for everyday life's simple joys and blessings. It's about pausing to savor the beauty of a sunset, the laughter of loved ones, or the taste of a delicious meal. By cultivating gratitude and appreciation, we can shift our perspective from scarcity to abundance, finding joy and fulfillment in the small moments that make life meaningful.

Don't forget that living in the present moment requires practicing self-compassion and self-care, nurturing our physical, emotional, and spiritual well-being with kindness and compassion. It's about honoring our needs and boundaries, setting aside time for rest, and engaging in activities that nourish our souls and replenish our energy. By prioritizing self-care and self-compassion, we can cultivate a deeper sense of inner peace and resilience, enabling us to navigate life's challenges with grace and poise.

Yes, living in the present moment requires practicing forgiveness and letting go of resentment and grudges from the past. It's about releasing the emotional baggage that weighs us down and embracing forgiveness as a path to healing and liberation. By letting go of the past and forgiving ourselves and others, we can experience greater peace and freedom in the present moment, fully embracing life with an open heart and a clear mind.

One aspect of living in the present moment is practicing mindfulness in our daily activities. Mindfulness involves bringing our full attention and awareness to the present moment, free from judgment or distraction. Whether eating a meal, taking a walk, or engaging in a conversation, mindfulness allows us to savor the richness of each experience, deepening our connection to ourselves and the world around us. Practicing mindfulness regularly can cultivate a greater sense of presence and aliveness in our lives, enhancing our overall well-being and quality of life.

Moreover, living in the present moment involves embracing uncertainty and the unknown as an inherent part of life's journey. It's about letting go of the need for certainty and control and learning to trust in the unfolding of life's mysteries. By embracing uncertainty, we can open ourselves up to new possibilities and opportunities, allowing life to surprise and delight us in unexpected ways. In doing so, we can experience greater freedom and spontaneity, living with a sense of adventure and curiosity about what each moment may bring.

In addition to embracing uncertainty, living in the present moment requires practicing acceptance and non-resistance to its reality. It's about acknowledging and embracing our experiences, both pleasant and unpleasant, without trying to change or resist them. We can reduce our suffering by accepting things and finding greater peace and contentment in the here and now. Acceptance allows us to let go of struggles and attachments, freeing ourselves to experience the richness of life in its entirety fully.

Furthermore, living now involves cultivating compassion and kindness towards ourselves and others. It's about approaching ourselves and others with empathy and understanding, recognizing our shared humanity and interconnectedness. By practicing compassion, we can cultivate deeper connections with others, fostering a sense of belonging and community. Compassion also allows us to extend forgiveness and grace to ourselves and others, promoting healing and reconciliation in our relationships.

How can you live in the moment, even in the face of external pressure or expectations? The answer is simple and clear. It's about being true to ourselves and honoring what truly matters to us, even in the face of external pressures or expectations. By living in alignment with our values, we can experience greater fulfillment and purpose in our lives, feeling a deep sense of satisfaction and meaning in our endeavors. Living authentically allows us to express ourselves fully and live with wholeness and integrity.

Ultimately, living in the present moment is a lifelong journey of self-discovery and growth, an invitation to awaken to the fullness and richness of life. By cultivating mindfulness, embracing uncertainty, practicing acceptance, and living with compassion, authenticity, and imperfection, we can experience greater joy, peace, and fulfillment in each moment. Living in the present moment allows us to fully engage with life, savoring its beauty and wonder and embracing the fullness of our humanity.

Making Positive Choices

Making positive choices is fundamental to leading a fulfilling and purposeful life. It involves conscious decision making aligning with one's values, goals, and well-being. Individuals can create a meaningful and satisfying life by making choices that promote personal growth, health, and positive relationships.

At its core, making positive choices requires self-awareness and reflection. It involves understanding one's values, goals, and priorities and using this understanding to guide decisions. By being mindful of what truly matters, individuals can make choices that support their long-term well-being and happiness. This self-awareness allows for more intentional living, where each decision is a step towards a more fulfilling life.

Yes, making positive choices involves considering the impact of decisions on one's physical and mental health. This means prioritizing habits and behaviors that promote wellbeing, such as maintaining a balanced diet, exercising regularly, and getting adequate rest. It also involves managing stress effectively, seeking support when needed, and engaging in activities that foster mental and emotional resilience. By prioritizing health, individuals can ensure that their choices contribute to their overall quality of life.

It is a dynamic process encompassing various aspects of life, including personal development, relationships, career, health, and community engagement. This holistic approach ensures that decisions contribute to a balanced, purposeful, and fulfilling existence.

An essential aspect of making positive choices is setting clear and achievable goals. Goal setting provides direction and motivation, helping individuals to stay focused on their aspirations. By breaking down larger goals into smaller, manageable steps, individuals can create a roadmap for success. This structured approach makes goals seem less daunting and provides a sense of accomplishment as each step is completed, reinforcing positive behavior.

Personal development often involves continuous self-improvement and learning. This can take many forms, such as pursuing further education, developing new skills, or engaging in self-reflection and mindfulness practices. Investing in personal growth not only enhances one's capabilities but also fosters a sense of confidence and self-efficacy. This proactive self-development approach ensures that individuals constantly evolve and adapt to new challenges and opportunities.

Positive choices in relationships require intentionality and effort. Building and maintaining healthy relationships involves effective communication, empathy, and mutual respect. It is important to choose supportive and nurturing relationships where both parties contribute positively to each other's lives. Investing time and energy into meaningful connections can lead to deeper, more fulfilling relationships. This might mean prioritizing quality time with loved ones, resolving conflicts constructively, and being present and attentive in interactions.

Health and wellness are integral to making positive choices. This includes not only physical health but also mental and emotional well-being. Making positive health choices involves regular exercise, a balanced diet, sufficient sleep, and proactive healthcare. It also includes managing stress through mindfulness practices, hobbies, and relaxation techniques. Mental health should be prioritized by seeking support when needed and practicing self-care. These choices contribute to overall well-being and enhance one's ability to handle life's challenges effectively.

Engaging in community and social responsibility is another important aspect of making positive choices. Contributing to the well-being of others and the community can take many forms, such as volunteering, participating in community projects, or advocating for social and environmental causes. These actions foster a sense of purpose and connection and help build a better society. Individuals can create a positive impact beyond their personal lives by making choices that benefit the greater good.

Financial decisions also play a significant role in making positive choices. This involves responsible resource management, planning for the future, and making informed decisions about spending, saving, and investing. Financial stability provides a foundation for other positive choices, reducing stress and enabling individuals to pursue their goals and aspirations more freely. Making conscious financial choices involves budgeting, avoiding unnecessary debt, and planning for long-term economic health.

Finally, making positive choices involves a commitment to self-compassion and forgiveness. Recognizing that no one is perfect and everyone makes mistakes is important. Self-compassion allows individuals to learn from their mistakes without self-criticism, fostering resilience and a positive mindset. Forgiveness, both of oneself and others, is crucial for moving forward and letting go of past grievances. This emotional maturity enhances one's ability to make positive choices consistently.

Affirming Your New Path

Affirming your new path is a multifaceted process encompassing various strategies and practices to ensure alignment with your true self and long-term goals. It involves cultivating self-belief, setting clear intentions, practicing positive reinforcement, fostering supportive relationships, embracing continuous learning, engaging in reflection, building resilience, and practicing self-compassion. Through these integrated approaches, you can strengthen your commitment to your new direction and navigate your journey confidently and purposefully.

At its core, affirming your new path begins with developing a strong sense of self-belief. Believing in your abilities and decisions builds resilience and perseverance in facing challenges. By cultivating confidence in your capacity to succeed, you empower yourself to overcome obstacles and pursue your goals with determination.

Setting clear intentions is essential for affirming your new path. Intentions are guiding principles that direct your actions and decisions toward your desired outcomes. By articulating what you want to achieve and why, you create a roadmap that helps you stay focused, motivated, and aligned with your purpose.

Positive reinforcement plays a crucial role in affirming your new path. Acknowledging and celebrating your progress and achievements boosts your confidence and reinforces your commitment to your goals. Regularly recognizing big and small wins encourages and motivates us to sustain momentum and overcome challenges.

Surrounding yourself with supportive relationships is another key aspect of affirming your new path. Seeking out individuals who share your values and aspirations can offer invaluable encouragement, advice, and accountability.

Building a network of support helps you navigate obstacles, celebrate successes, and stay committed to your journey.

Continuous learning and growth are integral to affirming your new path. Embracing personal and professional development opportunities allows you to expand your skills, knowledge, and perspectives. By staying curious and open to new experiences, you enhance your adaptability and resilience, ensuring you can navigate your journey with agility and confidence.

Reflection plays a vital role in affirming your new path. Regularly assessing your progress, strengths, and areas for improvement allows you to course-correct and stay aligned with your goals. Reflection deepens your self-awareness and helps you stay connected to your purpose, guiding your decisions and actions with greater clarity and intentionality.

Building resilience and perseverance are essential for affirming your new path. Embracing setbacks and challenges as opportunities for growth strengthens your resolve and determination. By cultivating resilience, you develop the resilience to bounce back from adversity and stay committed to your goals, even when the journey is challenging.

Practicing self-compassion is also crucial in affirming your new path. Treating yourself with kindness and understanding, especially in the face of setbacks or difficulties, fosters a positive mindset and reduces self-criticism. By practicing self-compassion, you cultivate the resilience and emotional well-being needed to navigate your journey with grace and authenticity.

In conclusion, affirming your new path is a holistic process that involves integrating various strategies and practices to align with your true self and long-term goals. By cultivating self-belief, setting clear intentions, practicing positive reinforcement, fostering supportive relationships, embracing continuous learning, engaging in reflection, building resilience, and practicing self-compassion, you can strengthen your commitment to your new direction and navigate your journey with confidence, purpose, and authenticity.

Declaring Freedom from the Past

Declaring freedom from the past is a multi-faceted journey that requires courage, self-compassion, and commitment. It involves acknowledging past experiences, reframing limiting beliefs, embracing vulnerability, practicing forgiveness, nurturing self-love, and cultivating gratitude. By integrating these practices into daily life, individuals can release the grip of past traumas, conditioning, and negative self-perceptions and step into a future filled with possibility, purpose, and authenticity.

At its core, declaring freedom from the past is about recognizing that the past does not define one's identity or determine one's future. It's about releasing attachments to past experiences and reframing them as opportunities for growth and learning. By letting go of regrets, resentments, and self-limiting beliefs, individuals can cultivate self-compassion and forgiveness, allowing them to move forward with clarity and intention.

It requires the courage to confront and heal old wounds. It involves acknowledging past traumas and pain without allowing them to define one's sense of worth or potential. Seeking support from trusted friends, family members, or professionals can provide guidance, validation, and encouragement, facilitating healing and paving the way for renewal.

Challenging and reframing limiting beliefs is another essential aspect of declaring freedom from the past. It's about recognizing and questioning negative thought patterns and replacing them with empowering beliefs that affirm one's worth, potential, and resilience. Individuals can overcome self-imposed limitations and embrace new opportunities for growth and fulfillment by cultivating a mindset of self-compassion, optimism, and possibility.

Also, declaring freedom from the past involves practicing mindfulness and presence in the present moment. It's about releasing attachments to past regrets or anxieties about the future and fully embracing the here and now. Mindfulness practices help individuals cultivate a sense of calm, clarity, and acceptance, allowing them to let go of past grievances and focus on creating a more fulfilling present and future.

Taking intentional actions that align with one's values, goals, and aspirations is also crucial in declaring freedom from the past. It involves making choices that honor one's authentic self and support one's journey of growth and self-discovery. This may include setting boundaries with toxic relationships or environments, pursuing new hobbies or interests, or seeking personal or professional development opportunities.

In short, declaring freedom from the past is a courageous self-liberation act involving releasing attachments to past experiences, healing old wounds, and embracing a future filled with possibility and purpose. By confronting past traumas, reframing limiting beliefs, practicing mindfulness, taking intentional actions, and cultivating self-love, forgiveness, and gratitude, individuals can reclaim their autonomy, heal emotional wounds, and create space for growth, resilience, and joy. Through intentional and mindful practice, individuals can declare their freedom from the limitations of the past and step into a brighter, more empowered future.

Encouragement for the Future

Encouragement for the future is a powerful message that uplifts individuals, instills hope, and inspires action toward realizing their dreams and aspirations. It serves as a beacon of light, guiding individuals through challenges and uncertainties and reminding them of their potential to create a brighter tomorrow. By offering encouragement for the future, individuals can cultivate resilience, optimism, and determination to overcome obstacles and pursue their goals with unwavering confidence.

One essential aspect of encouragement for the future is instilling belief in oneself and one's abilities. It's about reminding individuals of their inherent worth, talents, and capabilities and encouraging them to trust their capacity to overcome challenges and achieve success. By fostering self-belief, individuals can cultivate the confidence and resilience to navigate life's ups and downs with grace and determination.

It involves providing support and guidance to help individuals navigate their journey towards their goals. It's about offering encouragement, advice, and resources that empower individuals to overcome obstacles and seize opportunities for growth and development. By serving as a mentor or coach, individuals can provide valuable support and guidance that enables others to thrive and succeed.

Encouragement for the future also entails fostering a growth mindset that embraces challenges and sees failures as opportunities for learning and growth. It's about encouraging individuals to adopt a positive outlook on life, where setbacks are viewed as temporary rather than insurmountable obstacles. By promoting a growth mindset, individuals can cultivate resilience, perseverance, and adaptability, essential for navigating future uncertainties.

Don't forget to celebrate progress and achievements, no matter how small. It's about recognizing and affirming individuals' efforts and accomplishments, validating their hard work and dedication to their goals. By celebrating milestones, individuals can boost morale, motivation, and confidence, fueling further progress and success.

It entails fostering a sense of optimism and possibility. It's about inspiring individuals to dream big, set ambitious goals, and believe in the limitless potential of what they can achieve. By encouraging a positive outlook on the future, individuals can cultivate a sense of hope and excitement about what lies ahead, motivating them to pursue their aspirations with passion and determination.

How does the encouragement for the future entail a sense of community? Encouragement for the future involves fostering a sense of community and collaboration. It's about building networks of support and collaboration where individuals can share ideas, resources, and experiences and lift each other toward collective success. By fostering a sense of belonging and camaraderie, individuals can create a supportive environment where everyone feels empowered to pursue their goals and dreams.

Overall, encouragement for the future is a powerful message that uplifts individuals, instills hope, and inspires action toward realizing their dreams and aspirations. By fostering self-belief, providing support and guidance, promoting a growth mindset, celebrating progress and achievements, inspiring optimism and possibility, offering encouragement during adversity, and fostering a sense of community and collaboration, individuals can empower others to navigate the uncertainties of the future with confidence and resilience. Through intentional acts of encouragement, individuals can create a brighter tomorrow filled with endless possibilities and opportunities for growth and success.

7 PUT DOWN YOUR PHONE AND PICK UP YOUR BIBLE

In today's fast-paced world, it's all too easy to get swept up in the constant stream of notifications, messages, and updates from our smartphones and other digital devices. We're always connected to social media, the news, and various forms of entertainment. But it's crucial to remember the immense benefits of putting down our phones and giving ourselves a much-needed break from the digital realm. This disconnecting can inspire and motivate us, leading to a deeper connection with our spirituality. It's a moment of respite, a breath of fresh air in the digital storm, that can bring a profound sense of calm and reassurance.

"Life is happening outside the screen; don't miss it."

~How To Break Up With Your Phone - Bookey

Overindulging in social media can profoundly impact our mental health, productivity, and overall well-being. The constant comparison, anxiety, and distraction that come with evaluating our lives against the carefully curated images and experiences of our peers can be overwhelming. That's why it's crucial to step back, disconnect from our screens, and allow ourselves to rest, recharge, and reconnect with the real world. This break can bring a sense of relief, reducing the anxiety and pressure that social media often brings, and it's a break that we urgently need.

Digital Detox and Spiritual Reconnection

Devoting dedicated time to reading the Bible and communicating with God through prayer can fill us with His peace, wisdom, and guidance. These moments of quiet solitude with Him can bring a profound sense of calm, reassurance, and comfort, enveloping us in a soothing embrace that helps us navigate life's challenges with a clearer mind and a lighter heart.

Social media provides a constant stream of information, connection, and entertainment. However, excessive use of social media and phones can harm our mental health, productivity, and relationships. It's crucial to be mindful of our screen time and set healthy limits to ensure that these platforms don't overpower the more significant aspects of our lives. By taking control of our social media usage, we can regain a sense of empowerment and balance in our lives.

Finding comfort, direction, and nourishment in the words of the Bible through prayer and reading God's word is incredibly valuable, especially when compared to the constant noise and distractions of the digital world around us. When we unplug from our devices and make an effort to draw near to God, we can deepen our faith and gain a clearer understanding of our true purpose and calling in life.

In our busy, fast-paced world, we must take time each day to focus on God through prayer, meditation, or reading the Bible. These moments of solitude and communion with the divine can have a profound and transformative impact on our spiritual growth, inner peace, and overall well-being as we allow ourselves to be filled and refreshed by God's presence.

Our phones and digital devices always grab our attention with constant notifications, messages, and alerts. This endless demand for our focus can pull us away from more meaningful and essential things in life. We must set firm boundaries around our phone and device usage and choose to prioritize uninterrupted time spent in God's presence, where we can quiet our hearts and minds to hear better His still, small voice speaking wisdom and love to us.

Overcoming Digital Obsession

There was a time in my life when I was consumed by my obsession with watching YouTube. I would spend hours upon hours scrolling through videos, filling my head with nonsense and neglecting the essential relationships in my life.

In particular, I was putting YouTube over my relationship with my fiancé, forgetting to spend quality time with her and prioritizing online content over real-life connections. It took a wake-up call for me to realize the damage I was causing and to make a change for the better, overcoming a YouTube obsession and re-prioritizing my family values.

I remember the days when I would habitually reach for my phone when I woke up, immediately immersing myself in the endless scroll of YouTube's recommended video feed. I often spent hours completely enthralled, losing myself in endless digital entertainment and distractions.

This obsessive YouTube habit had become so ingrained that I seriously neglected my real-world responsibilities and the needs of the people closest to me. My caring fiancé would make attempts to engage with me, but I would callously brush her off, my attention entirely captivated by the alluring glow of the screen.

As my unhealthy fixation with YouTube content consumption grew increasingly problematic, I found myself spending less and less quality, meaningful time with my fiancé.

We used to enjoy deep, thoughtful conversations and cherish precious moments of intimate connection together. Still, now I was far too preoccupied with mindlessly scrolling and passively absorbing endless digital diversions to devote the care and attention my partner deserved. I was recklessly filling my mind with trivial entertainment and ephemeral pleasures from YouTube while tragically neglecting the nourishing bonds of our real-life relationship.

My fiancé gradually began to feel painfully lonely, overlooked, and unimportant as the distance and disconnect in our once vibrant partnership worsened.

Ultimately, my fiancé mustered the courage to have a problematic, heartfelt discussion with me. She vulnerably expressed her profound feelings of loneliness and emotional abandonment, making it clear how deeply my obsessive YouTube habits had wounded our relationship. This harsh, sobering reality check was exactly what I needed to finally snap out of my digital stupor and reevaluate my skewed life priorities.

Like so many others grappling with the addictive allure of modern technology, I had found myself wasting countless precious hours mindlessly consuming content on these online platforms, with little to show for it in terms of personal growth, meaning, or fulfillment. It wasn't until I recognized that the swift passage of time was leaving me behind, missing out on authentic human connections and opportunities for self- improvement, that I knew I had to make a dramatic change.

Balancing Screen Time

I consciously decided to limit my time on social media and YouTube, focusing instead on cutting back on my social media and YouTube usage. Instead, I focused my time and energy on enriching activities that nourished my mind, body, and soul.

I immersed myself in thought-provoking books, diving deep into stories and ideas that challenged and inspired me. I also incorporated more intentional prayer and meditation practices, seeking divine guidance and inner peace amidst the chaos of daily life.

As I carefully cultivated this renewed sense of balance, I discovered the profound impact of consuming uplifting and encouraging content. I started watching faith-based and motivational videos on YouTube, which filled my mind and spirit with positivity, hope, and a more profound sense of purpose. These videos entertained and empowered me to live more intentionally and meaningfully.

As I found greater harmony and equilibrium in my life, I noticed a marked shift in my overall well-being and outlook. I felt more grounded, focused, and at peace with myself and my circumstances. I could better prioritize my time and energy on what mattered to me, leading to greater fulfillment and satisfaction.

Maintaining balance is an ongoing, dynamic journey, especially in a world constantly bombarding us with distractions and temptations. I've learned the importance of setting healthy boundaries, practicing self-discipline, and staying true to my core values and beliefs. I can continue to navigate this path toward a balanced and purposeful life by remaining mindful and intentional about how I spend my time and energy.

Finding balance in life requires deep self-awareness, intentionality, and perseverance. By prioritizing activities and practices that nourish our minds, bodies, and souls, we can create a fulfilling and meaningful life that aligns with our deepest values and beliefs. Embarking on this journey toward balance and wholeness is a continuous and rewarding pursuit always within our reach.

In today's fast-paced, hyper-connected digital age, it's all too easy to become consumed by the endless scroll of social media, the constant notifications, and the never-ending stream of content that bombards us from our devices. But we must remember that life is happening outside the screen, and if we're not careful, we might miss the richness and beauty of the present moment.

Social media can often lead us down a path of comparison and discontent, fostering feelings of inadequacy, jealousy, and a distorted sense of self-worth. We must remember that our true worth and identity come not from the likes, comments, or validation of others but from our relationship with our Creator and the inherent value that He has bestowed upon us.

The timeless wisdom and guidance found within the pages of the Bible can be a profound source of comfort, inspiration, and transformation. By prioritizing time immersed in the Word of God, we can deepen our understanding of His character, promises, and will for our lives. The more we invest in this sacred text, the more we will be transformed and renewed in our faith, empowered to live with greater purpose and intention.

Speaking from personal experience, I can attest to the detrimental effects that excessive screen time and digital habits can have on our mental health, our relationships, and our overall well-being. The consequences of too much time spent on our phones and devices are far-reaching, from decreased productivity and increased anxiety to strained interpersonal connections and feelings of loneliness and isolation. We must recognize the significant impact of our digital choices and take intentional steps to reduce screen time and cultivate a healthier, more balanced relationship with technology.

Finding Peace

Breaking up with your phone doesn't mean completely disconnecting from the digital world. It means finding a healthy balance between screen time and real-life experiences. I've learned practical tips on reducing phone usage, setting technology boundaries, and prioritizing reallife interactions. From turning off notifications to setting designated phone-free times, plenty of strategies help you break free from your phone addiction and experience the joy of finding peace in the present moment.

I realized once you've successfully broken up with your phone, it's time to start embracing the world around you. Whether it's spending quality time with loved ones, pursuing a hobby, or simply enjoying the beauty of nature, there are countless ways to find joy and peace in real-life experiences. Focusing on the present moment and fully engaging in your surroundings can create meaningful memories and help you live a more fulfilling, purpose-driven life.

I wanted to be honest and share my experience of how too much phone time caused trouble in many areas of my life and how I successfully broke up with my phone and experienced positive changes. From spending more time reading and studying the Bible to rediscovering a love for nature and finding peace in my spirituality, I hope my personal stories inspire anyone looking to prioritize real-life experiences over screen time.

Life happens outside the screen, and it's up to us to make the most of it. We can create a more meaningful and fulfilling life by breaking up with our phones and embracing the world. Don't let life pass you by—take control of your screen time and start living in the present moment. Remember, the best moments in life are the ones that happen offline, where we can genuinely connect with others and find purpose.

I knew I needed to make a change to salvage my relationship and prioritize my family values. I started by setting boundaries for myself when it came to watching YouTube. I limited my screen time and consciously tried to spend more quality time with my fiancé. We went on dates, had meaningful conversations, and reconnected deeper. I realized that the absolute joy of finding peace comes from nurturing relationships and creating lasting memories, not mindlessly scrolling through online content.

Today, I am proud to say that I have overcome my YouTube obsession and re-prioritized my family values. My relationship with my fiancé is stronger than ever, and we make it a point to spend quality time together daily. I have learned the importance of balance and moderation in technology and found fulfillment in nurturing real-life connections. I hope my story reminds others struggling with similar obsessions that there is always a way to find balance and prioritize what truly matters.

I remember being obsessed with watching YouTube, but I am grateful for the wake-up call that helped me reevaluate my priorities and reprioritize my family values. I have rediscovered the joy of meaningful connections and quality time with my loved ones by overcoming my obsession and finding peace in my relationships.

My journey inspires others to step back from distractions and focus on what truly matters. Remember, family values should always come first, and alone time with God should strengthen your spirituality daily.

The first step in finding peace with God is to create a sacred space for yourself. This space should be free from distractions like cell phones and television. Find a quiet corner of your home where you can sit comfortably and be alone with God. Light a candle or burn incense to create a peaceful, contemplative atmosphere.

Make sure you are comfortable, whether sitting in a chair or on a cushion on the floor. This space should allow you to relax and focus on connecting with God more profoundly and meaningfully.

To truly connect with God, it is essential to let go of distractions. This means turning off your cell phone, putting away any work or household tasks, and turning off the television. Allow yourself to be fully present in the moment without any outside interruptions. This may be difficult at first, but with practice, you will find that you can let go of these distractions and focus solely on your time with God to find inner peace and spiritual fulfillment.

Listening to God's Voice

Once you've set aside a quiet, distraction-free space and cleared your cluttered mind, sit in reflective silence and listen intently for God's gentle, guiding voice. This may initially feel unfamiliar and uncomfortable if you're accustomed to constant noise and activity. Still, the profound silence allows you to deeply connect with God and discern his wisdom for your life. Take some slow, deep cleansing breaths and intentionally relax your body and mind into the peaceful, prayerful quiet. You can start by offering a brief prayer or reflecting on an inspirational Bible verse to help focus and center your spirit.

As you sit in the sacred silence, pay thoughtful attention to any insightful thoughts, stirring emotions, or subtle impressions that come to you. God may speak to you through his Spirit, offering timely wisdom, reassurance, or direction. Be open and receptive to hearing his voice, even if it doesn't align with your expectations or preferences.

God communicates with us in diverse and mysterious ways, so you must learn to discern his guidance amidst the clamor of daily life carefully. Trust wholeheartedly that God has a perfect purpose for you and will lead you along the right path if you remain attentive to his leading.

Remember that this contemplative, unhurried time with God is a precious opportunity to experience his comforting presence and find spiritual renewal for your weary soul. Deliberately let go and rest securely in the warm embrace of his boundless love. This is a sacred, set-apart time to recharge your spirit and deepen your relationship with the divine.

Make this time with your Creator a top priority, free from the constant demands and distractions of the world. Take comfort in knowing God is always with you amid relentless chaos and turbulence. Find your true peace, strength, and security in his steadfast companionship, trusting with unwavering certainty that you are never alone.

Cultivating this peace and connection with God is essential for spiritual well-being and growth. Intentionally creating a sacred space, setting aside distractions, sitting in respectful silence, and attentively listening for God's gentle voice are vital disciplines that will help you continually deepen your relationship and find unshakable comfort in his constant presence.

Remember to consistently prioritize time with your Creator, free from the overwhelming demands of everyday life. Trust that God faithfully guides and sustains you, and embrace the profound peace of spending meaningful time in communion with the divine.

Prioritizing Spiritual Well-Being

We must sit still and listen to God's voice for our spiritual growth and well-being. Understanding the importance of remaining steadfast in our faith, making a conscious decision to put God first over our phones, and the benefits of reading our Bibles regularly can help us embark on a journey to embrace the peace of time alone with God.

In a constantly changing world, losing sight of our faith and becoming distracted by the chaos can be easy. However, remaining steadfast and unwavering in our beliefs and trusting God's plan is crucial. We can find peace, strength, and stability in life's challenges by staying firmly rooted in our faith.

Taking the time to quiet our active minds and open our hearts can help us hear God's voice more clearly. We can cultivate a deeper, more intimate relationship with Him by setting aside dedicated time each day to sit still, reflect, and meditate on God's word.

God speaks to us in many profound and meaningful ways, but we must be willing and attentive enough to listen. By intentionally quieting our minds and hearts, we can tune into God's voice and receive His guidance, wisdom, and direction. Through fervent prayer, deep meditation, or immersive scripture study, we can discern God's voice and follow His will for our lives.

Cell phones and other digital devices can be constant distractions and temptations, pulling our attention away from what truly matters. However, we must consciously and deliberately prioritize our time with God over our devices. By setting healthy boundaries and making God the central focus of our lives, we can experience a profound sense of peace, purpose, and fulfillment.

The Bible is a powerful, transformative tool for spiritual growth and development. Regularly reading and meditating on God's word can provide invaluable insight, wisdom, and encouragement. The Bible is a wellspring of comfort, guidance, and hope, and by immersing ourselves in its timeless teachings, we can draw ever closer to God's heart.

"A Bible that's falling apart usually belongs to someone who isn't."
-Charles Spurgeon

Embracing peaceful, uninterrupted time with God is essential for our spiritual well-being and ongoing transformation. By remaining steadfast in our faith, sitting still, listening attentively to God's voice, prioritizing Him over our phones, and reading our Bibles faithfully, we can cultivate a deeper, more intimate relationship with our Heavenly Father. Let us consciously spend quality time with God and experience the profound peace and presence that flows from His loving embrace.

In a world constantly buzzing with noise, demands, and distractions, let's carve out sacred, uninterrupted time to focus on what truly matters most - our relationship with the Lord. Let's prioritize our time with God and give ourselves the precious gift of a break from the relentless pull of our phones and devices. Doing so can free our minds, nourish our souls, and draw us closer to the One who loves us with everlasting love.

Let's intentionally choose to put down our phones and immerse ourselves in God's word a few days a week. Let's dive deep into the pages of our Bibles, allowing God's truth to speak powerfully to our hearts. Let's create stillness and solitude, where we can listen intently to His voice and be refreshed, renewed, and recharged in His gentle, loving presence.

So, take a deep, cleansing breath, place your phone aside, and open your Bible. Spend precious, uninterrupted time alone with God, allowing His perfect peace to wash over you and His life-giving truth to revive your weary spirit. In these sacred moments of stillness and connection, you will find the rest, rejuvenation, and spiritual nourishment your soul profoundly craves.

8 PAIN INTO PURPOSE

I spent many years trapped in addiction, crime, and causing pain to myself and those around me. Eventually, I realized that my suffering had a greater purpose. Pain is a universal experience that can lead to growth and transformation when embraced and learned from. Through my darkest times, including nights in jail, I found strength in faith and the unwavering prayers of my great-grandmother.

> *"Hurt often holds the hidden key to unlocking your most incredible healing."*
> *~Brittany Burgunder*

By turning to God and seeking His guidance, I began to see my life in a new light. My past mistakes became tools to help others facing similar struggles. Sharing my story has allowed me to inspire and support others, turning my pain into a source of strength and resilience. Trusting God's plan and finding purpose in my struggles transformed my life. I now use my experiences to offer hope and encouragement to those in need, showing there is always a way out, even in the darkest moments. My journey from darkness to light demonstrates the power of faith, forgiveness, and redemption.

From Pain to Purpose: Traversing the Journey of Redemption

The path from pain to purpose is a transformative journey that has redefined my existence. This heading embodies the profound shift from enduring immense suffering to discovering a higher calling through redemption. It encapsulates that pain, no matter how intense, can catalyze significant personal growth and a deeper connection to one's purpose.

My journey began in a place of deep anguish, where addiction, crime, and self-destructive behaviors dominated my life. I inflicted pain upon myself and those around me, trapped in a cycle that seemed impossible to break. My actions caused immeasurable hurt to my family, community, and soul. I was lost in a dark abyss, unable to see any way out.

However, a glimmer of hope emerged in the depths of my despair. This hope was not immediate or all-encompassing; it was a small, persistent light that gradually grew stronger. It started with a realization that my life had to change and that redemption and transformation were possible. The first steps were the hardest: admitting my faults, seeking forgiveness, and confronting the pain head-on.

As I embarked on this journey of redemption, I discovered that pain could be an influential teacher. It forced me to look inward, examine the root causes of my actions, and understand the deeper wounds that had led me astray. Through this introspection, I began to see pain not as an enemy but as a guide that could lead me toward healing and growth.

Turning to faith played a crucial role in my transformation. I found solace and strength in prayer, meditation, and spiritual practices that helped me connect with a higher power. This connection provided me with the guidance and support I desperately needed. Through faith, I understood that my suffering had a purpose and could be used for something greater than myself.

Redemption also involved making amends and seeking forgiveness. I reached out to those I had hurt, offering sincere apologies and striving to repair the damage I had done. This process was humbling and deeply challenging, but it was also liberating. Each reconciliation brought me closer to a sense of peace and wholeness, reinforcing the transformative power of grace.

In finding my purpose, I realized that my experiences could serve as a beacon of hope for others. By sharing my story, I could inspire and support those navigating their journeys through pain and hardship. My past, once a source of shame, became a testament to the resilience of the human spirit and the possibility of redemption.

This journey from pain to purpose is ongoing. It requires continual self-reflection, faith, and a commitment to living authentically. My story is about overcoming adversity and using those experiences to impact the world positively. By turning my pain into a source of strength and inspiration, I have found a more profound sense of purpose that guides me daily.

Traversing the journey of redemption has shown me that no matter how deep the suffering is, there is always the potential for transformation. I have discovered a path to a more meaningful and fulfilling life by embracing my pain, seeking forgiveness, and finding my purpose. My journey is a testament to the power of faith, resilience, and the enduring human capacity for redemption.

Embracing the Crucible: Finding Strength in Adversity

Embracing pain and finding strength in vulnerability has been a cornerstone of my transformative journey. This heading highlights the paradoxical power of acknowledging and accepting pain to discover profound inner strength and resilience. It speaks to the necessity of facing my deepest wounds and fears to emerge more substantial and authentic.

For much of my life, I perceived pain as an adversary to be avoided at all costs. The agony of addiction, the shame of my actions, and the emotional scars I carried seemed insurmountable. I masked my suffering with destructive behaviors, pushing away the very feelings that demanded my attention. However, this avoidance deepened my despair and prolonged my journey through darkness.

The turning point came when I realized that true healing required me to confront my pain head-on. I had to dismantle the walls I had built around my heart and allow myself to be vulnerable. This was a challenging task. Allowing myself to feel the total weight of my emotions, to sit with my sorrow and regret, was excruciating. Yet, I discovered a wellspring of strength hidden beneath the surface of this vulnerability.

Embracing pain meant acknowledging my mistakes and the harm I had caused. It required me to take responsibility for my actions and to seek forgiveness, not only from others but also from myself. This process was profoundly humbling as it laid bare my flaws and imperfections. However, through this humility, I began to rebuild my life on a foundation of honesty and integrity.

Vulnerability also opened the door to profound connections with others. By sharing my struggles and being open about my journey, I found a community of support that

I had never known before. People responded to my honesty with compassion and understanding, creating a network of relationships built on mutual respect and empathy. This sense of connection provided the strength I needed to continue my path to recovery.

In my vulnerability, I also discovered the importance of self-care and compassion. I learned to treat myself with the kindness and understanding I readily extended to others. This shift in perspective allowed me to heal the wounds of my past and nurture my emotional and mental well-being. By prioritizing self-care, I equipped myself with the tools to face future challenges with resilience and grace.

Turning to my faith, I found solace in believing that my pain had a purpose. Spiritual practices like prayer and meditation became crucial in helping me process my emotions and find peace amidst the chaos. Through faith, I began to understand that my vulnerability was not a sign of weakness but a testament to my strength and courage. Through this lens, I started to see my struggles as opportunities for growth and transformation.

Embracing pain and finding strength in vulnerability has been a profound and ongoing journey. It has taught me that true resilience is born from facing my deepest fears and accepting myself wholly, with all my flaws and strengths. My story is a testament to the power of vulnerability, illustrating that I have found an inner strength that has transformed my life through embracing pain.

This journey has shown me that vulnerability is not a liability but a powerful tool for healing and connection. By embracing my pain and allowing myself to be vulnerable, I have discovered a more profound sense of purpose and authenticity. My experiences have shaped me into a stronger, more compassionate individual, and I hope my journey can inspire others to find their strength in vulnerability.

The Power of Faith Amidst Darkness: A Beacon of Hope

The power of faith amidst darkness has been a guiding beacon of hope in my life, illuminating the path through some of my most challenging times. This heading encapsulates how faith has served as a source of light and strength, helping me navigate through the shadows of addiction, despair, and self- destruction.

In the darkest periods of my life, I was overwhelmed by the consequences of my actions. Addiction had taken its toll, leaving me in a state of constant turmoil and hopelessness. The pain I inflicted upon myself and others seemed impossible, and I often questioned whether there was any way out of the abyss I had created. During these moments of profound despair, I discovered the transformative power of faith.

My journey towards faith began subtly, with the persistent prayers of my great-grandmother. Her unwavering belief in my potential, even when I had lost all hope in myself, planted the seeds of faith within me. Initially, these seeds lay dormant, overshadowed by my struggles and doubts. However, as I started to open my heart to the possibility of redemption, these seeds grew, nurtured by the gentle light of faith.

Turning to faith did not provide immediate relief from my suffering, but it offered a sense of purpose and direction that I desperately needed. Prayer and meditation became essential, allowing me to find peace and clarity amidst the chaos. Through prayer, I communicated my fears, regrets, and hopes to a higher power, finding solace in surrendering my burdens. Meditation helped me stay present, preventing my thoughts from spiraling into darkness.

As I deepened my faith, I began to perceive my pain differently. Instead of seeing it as an enemy, I started to view it as a catalyst for growth and transformation. Faith taught me that my struggles were not in vain; they shaped me into a more resilient and compassionate individual. This realization was empowering, as it gave meaning to my suffering and provided a sense of hope for the future.

One of the most significant aspects of faith was its ability to connect me with a supportive community. Sharing my journey with others who had faced similar challenges reinforced my belief in the power of faith to heal and transform lives. This sense of belonging and mutual support was crucial in my recovery, offering encouragement and accountability as I navigated my path to redemption.

Faith also introduced me to forgiveness—self-forgiveness and seeking forgiveness from those I had wronged. This process was profoundly humbling but also incredibly liberating. It allowed me to release the heavy burden of guilt and shame that I had been carrying, making space for healing and renewal. Through faith, I learned that forgiveness was not a sign of weakness but a testament to the strength of the human spirit.

Today, faith remains a beacon of hope, guiding me through the inevitable ups and downs. It reminds me that even in the darkest moments, there is a light that can lead me towards redemption and peace. The power of faith has transformed my life, turning my pain into a source of strength and resilience. It has shown me that no matter how deep the darkness is, there is always a beacon of hope to guide me towards the light.

My journey is a testament to faith's profound impact amidst darkness. It illustrates that I found the strength and courage to overcome my past and embrace a future filled with hope and purpose through faith. Faith has been my guiding light, illuminating the path toward healing and redemption, and it continues to inspire me to live a life of meaning and fulfillment.

Finding Strength in Vulnerability: Embracing Emotional Healing

One of the most profound lessons I've learned in the complex journey of healing is the strength that lies within vulnerability. This heading captures the essence of acknowledging and embracing my emotions as a vital part of the healing process. It suggests that true strength isn't about hiding my pain or putting on a brave face but about allowing myself to be open, honest, and vulnerable in the face of adversity.

Embracing vulnerability means confronting my pain head- on rather than suppressing it or pretending it doesn't exist. It involves leaning into my emotions, feeling them fully, and understanding that this process is crucial to healing. Through vulnerability, I unlock the doors to emotional growth and resilience, discovering a depth of strength I never knew I possessed.

In my darkest moments, I found that allowing myself to be vulnerable was not a sign of weakness but a testament to my courage. It required immense bravery to face my inner demons, acknowledge my fears and insecurities, and share my struggles with others. I was doing so created space for genuine emotional healing, breaking free from denial and repression.

The power of vulnerability lies in its ability to foster deep connections and understanding. When I open up about my pain and struggles, I invite others to do the same, creating a supportive and empathetic community. This shared vulnerability becomes a source of collective strength, where I find solace in knowing I am not alone in my experiences.

It is in these moments of shared humanity that true healing begins.

Embracing vulnerability also means recognizing the importance of self-care and seeking support when needed. It involves prioritizing my emotional well-being, whether through therapy, meditation, or leaning on loved ones for support. By taking these steps, I acknowledge that my emotional health is just as important as my physical health and that seeking help is a courageous act of self-love.

Through my journey, I've understood that vulnerability is a powerful catalyst for personal growth and transformation. It allows me to shed the layers of pretense and embrace my authentic self, with all its imperfections and scars. In doing so, I discover inner peace and strength that empowers me to navigate life's challenges with grace and resilience.

It reminds me that finding strength in vulnerability is crucial to healing. By embracing my emotions, seeking support, and allowing myself to be seen, I pave the way for profound emotional healing. In this journey of vulnerability, I find the courage to transform my pain into a source of strength and resilience, emerging as a stronger, more authentic version of myself.

Turning Pain into Purpose: Inspiring and Helping Others

The concept of transforming personal pain into a meaningful purpose is both empowering and transformative. This heading captures the essence of using my struggles and hardships as a catalyst for positive change, not just within myself but in the lives of others as well. It speaks to the idea that my experiences, no matter how painful, can serve a higher purpose by inspiring and helping those who face similar challenges.

Throughout my journey, I've understood that my pain holds a unique power. It has shaped, molded, and given me insights that can be invaluable to others. By sharing my story, I offer hope to those lost in their struggles, showing them that healing and redemption are possible. This sharing is about recounting my experiences and connecting with others on a deep, empathetic level.

Transforming pain into purpose begins with acknowledging and owning my past. It's about recognizing the lessons my struggles have taught me and understanding that these lessons can guide and uplift others. By being open about my journey, I can help break the stigma surrounding issues like addiction, depression, and emotional trauma, encouraging others to seek help and find their paths to recovery.

One of the most profound ways to find meaning in my pain is by using it to support and uplift others. I can offer encouragement and inspiration through writing, speaking, or simply being a listening ear. My story becomes a testament to the resilience of the human spirit, a reminder that no matter how deep the darkness is, there is always a path to the light.

Helping others through my experiences also brings a sense of fulfillment and purpose. It transforms my pain from something that once felt isolating and insurmountable into a powerful tool for good. By turning my past struggles into a source of strength, I heal myself and create positivity and hope in the world around me.

Moreover, turning pain into purpose allows me to live authentically and intentionally. It guides my decisions, fuels my passions, and shapes my interactions with others. By aligning my actions with this newfound purpose, I create a meaningful and impactful life where my past is not a burden but a beacon of hope and transformation.

It is a call to action to embrace my pain, not as a source of shame or regret, but as a powerful instrument for change. By sharing my journey and using my experiences to help others, I find a sense of purpose that transcends my healing. In turning pain into purpose, I transform my life and become a source of inspiration and hope for countless others, proving that the most profound strengths can come from the deepest struggles.

9 WALK OF FAITH

"I have learned that while speaking about one's miseries usually hurts, those who keep silent hurt more." ~C. S. Lewis

In the past, I sometimes gossiped and criticized others, which I now realize was harmful. I've learned the importance of being more thoughtful and compassionate in my interactions. However, many painful experiences humbled me and made me confront my shortcomings. I struggled with addiction, life on the streets, and sex addiction, but through God's grace and the support of NA, I turned my life around. I use my story to help others facing similar challenges, showing the power of faith and redemption.

Living on the streets was harsh, but God guided me toward a better path. Overcoming sex addiction through prayer and counseling, I found healing and forgiveness. I felt responsible for sharing my story, offering hope and inspiration to those struggling.

Today, I am free from addiction. Trusting in God's love and grace, I found a new purpose. If you are struggling, know there is hope. Trust in God and believe in yourself. In my faith journey, I realized the immense love and grace God has given me. This inspired me to give back and share my faith with conviction and passion through acts of kindness and my testimony. My trials led to a deeper understanding of God's love. By sharing my story, I inspire others to find healing and wholeness.

Our words can heal or harm. We can positively impact the world by speaking with kindness, empathy, and compassion. My journey shows that while pain is inevitable, growth and healing are always possible. Let us be sources of light and love, choosing to heal and offer hope to those in need.

From Gossip to Grace: My Transformation

There was a time when I thrived on gossip and criticism, reveling in the miseries of others without understanding the damage I was inflicting. I eagerly discussed others' problems, finding a twisted pleasure in their struggles. Little did I know that this behavior reflected my insecurities and shortcomings. It took a series of humbling and painful experiences for me to see the error of my ways.

God intervened in my life in ways I couldn't ignore. Through these trials, I was forced to confront my flaws and the harmful impact of my words. It was a complex process, but it led to a profound transformation. I realized that strength and character come from lifting others, not tearing them down.

I discovered gossip and criticism were coping mechanisms for my unhappiness and dissatisfaction. As I worked through my issues, I found a new purpose: to become a source of inspiration and support for others. Instead of indulging in harmful talk, I chose to speak words of encouragement and hope.

This journey from gossip to grace was challenging. It required deep introspection and a willingness to change. I had to face the harsh reality that my words could either build people up or break them down. Recognizing this, I started to cultivate a habit of empathy and compassion, aiming to understand others rather than judge them. This shift in perspective was both liberating and empowering.

Through prayer and reflection, I gained insights into my vulnerabilities and began to heal from past wounds. I realized my tendency to gossip was rooted in my pain and the need for validation. As I embraced God's love and grace, I learned to find my worth in Him rather than in the fleeting satisfaction of tearing others down.

My relationships began to change as well. Friends and family noticed the difference in my attitude and approach. Instead of being the person who spread negativity, I became someone people could confide in and trust. I started to see the impact of my words in a new light. A kind word, a listening ear, or a supportive comment could make a world of difference to someone in need.

The transformation also extended to how I viewed my purpose in life. I felt a calling to use my experiences to help struggling others. Whether it was someone dealing with addiction, battling self-esteem issues, or simply needing a friend, I wanted to be there for them. I found fulfillment in being a light source in a world often overshadowed by darkness.

This change didn't happen overnight. It was a continuous process of growth and learning. There were setbacks and moments of doubt, but each step forward brought me closer to the person I wanted to be. I understood that grace wasn't just something I received; I could extend it to others through my words and actions.

Today, I look back on my journey with gratitude. What once was a source of shame has become a testimony to the transformative power of grace. I am committed to speaking life and positivity into the lives of those around me. My transformation from gossip to grace reminds me that change is possible and that our words hold the power to heal and uplift.

In sharing my story, I inspire others to reflect on their words' impact and choose grace over gossip. We all can grow and change to become sources of hope and encouragement in a desperately needy world. We can transform our lives and those around us through faith, introspection, and a commitment to positivity.

Overcoming Addiction: A Journey of Faith and Redemption

Addiction is a relentless force, one that grips the mind and soul; escaping seems impossible. For years, I was trapped in the vice of addiction, each day a battle against cravings and the haunting pull of substances. My life spiraled out of control, and I found myself on the streets, drowning in a sea of despair. I struggled not only with drug addiction but also with sex addiction, each compounding my feelings of shame and hopelessness.

The turning point came when I hit rock bottom. I realized I could not overcome these battles alone in this abyss of darkness. In my desperation, I turned to God, seeking solace and guidance. Prayer became my lifeline, and I felt a glimmer of hope. Faith became my anchor, grounding me when the storms of withdrawal and temptation threatened to overwhelm me.

The journey to recovery was far from easy. Withdrawal brought intense physical and emotional pain, pushing me to the brink. Yet, with each prayer, I found a new strength, a resilience I had never known. God's grace provided the fortitude I needed to face my demons head-on and to persevere through the most challenging moments.

The support of Narcotics Anonymous (NA) was instrumental in my recovery. Surrounded by others who understood my struggles, I found a community providing support and accountability. Sharing my story in NA meetings, I realized that my experiences could be a beacon of hope for others. My pain and struggles had a purpose: to help others find their path to healing.

Living on the streets had taught me harsh lessons about survival, but through faith, I learned about redemption and the possibility of a new beginning. God's love was a constant presence, guiding me toward a better path. The kindness of strangers and the unwavering support of my faith community helped me leave the streets behind and start anew.

Overcoming sex addiction required confronting deep-seated issues and facing the shame that had kept me trapped for so long. Through prayer and counseling, I found the courage to confront these issues and seek forgiveness. God's love and grace offered a path to healing and self-acceptance, allowing me to rebuild my life based on faith and purity.

Throughout this journey, I have learned the power of faith and the importance of perseverance. Each setback allowed me to lean more deeply into my faith and trust God's plan. The journey was arduous, but each step forward was a testament to the transformative power of grace.

Today, I stand free from the chains of addiction, filled with a sense of purpose and direction. My life is now dedicated to helping others struggling with similar issues. By sharing my story, I inspire others to seek help and to believe in the possibility of redemption. There is hope, even in the darkest moments, and it is possible to overcome the most formidable challenges with faith.

My journey from addiction to redemption is a testament to the power of faith and the unyielding grace of God. It reminds me that no matter how deep the despair, there is always a path to healing and wholeness. By embracing faith and seeking support, I was able to reclaim my life and find a new purpose. I am living proof that recovery is possible, and I am committed to sharing this message of hope with anyone who needs it.

Finding Strength in the Depths of Despair

In the depths of despair, I discovered a reservoir of strength I never knew I possessed. Life had pushed me to my breaking point, and I found myself teetering on the edge of hopelessness. Addiction had consumed me, dragging me down a dark and lonely path. Each day felt like a battle for survival, and the weight of my struggles threatened to crush me.

But in those darkest moments, something remarkable happened. I tapped into a wellspring of inner resilience that I never knew existed. It was a resilience forged in the fires of adversity, tempered by hardship and pain. Despite the overwhelming odds stacked against me, I found the courage to keep fighting and pushing forward, no matter how futile it seemed.

During my lowest moments, I realized the actual depth of my strength. I had endured hardships that would have broken others, yet I refused to let them define me. Instead, I drew upon my inner reserves of courage and determination, using them as a lifeline to cling to in the storm.

Through prayer and reflection, I found solace in chaos. God became my rock, my refuge in times of trouble. His presence gave me the strength and comfort I needed to endure even the darkest days. With each whispered prayer, I felt His guiding hand leading me forward, showing me I was never alone.

As I navigated the treacherous waters of addiction and despair, I discovered a newfound sense of purpose. My struggles imbued me with empathy and understanding for others facing similar battles. I realized that my pain had a purpose and that my experiences could be a source of inspiration and hope for struggling people.

Through acts of kindness and compassion, I found meaning while suffering. Whether lending a listening ear to a friend in need or offering a helping hand to a stranger, I discovered that even the smallest gestures could make a difference. In reaching out to others, I found a sense of connection and belonging that helped to alleviate the loneliness and isolation I had felt for so long.

My journey through despair has taught me valuable lessons about the resilience of the human spirit. I have learned that there is always hope, even in the darkest times. By tapping into our inner strength and drawing upon the support of others, we can overcome even the most insurmountable obstacles.

Today, I stand as a living testament to the power of resilience and faith. I have emerged from the depths of despair stronger and more determined than ever. My struggles have not defined me; they have shaped me into who I am today. I am grateful for the challenges I have faced, for they have taught me invaluable lessons about the strength of the human spirit and the power of hope.

Living with Purpose:
Turning Misery into Ministry

In the depths of my misery, I found a calling that would transform my life. For too long, I had been trapped in a cycle of self-destructive behavior, unable to see a way out of the darkness that consumed me. Addiction, despair, and shame clouded my vision, leaving me feeling lost and alone. But in my despair, a flicker of hope began to emerge.

As I grappled with my demons, I began to see my struggles in a new light. Instead of viewing them as obstacles to be overcome, I saw them as opportunities for growth and redemption. I realized that my pain had a purpose and that my experiences could help others facing similar battles.

With this newfound perspective, I embarked on a journey to turn my misery into ministry. I sought ways to share my story with others, offering them hope and encouragement in their struggles. Whether it was through volunteering at a local shelter, speaking at recovery meetings, or simply being a supportive friend, I embraced every opportunity to make a positive impact.

Living with purpose gave me a sense of direction and fulfillment that I had never known before. Instead of wallowing in self-pity, I found joy in serving others and making a difference in their lives. My past mistakes no longer weighed me down; they became stepping stones toward a brighter future.

Through my ministry, I discovered the power of empathy and compassion. I learned to listen without judgment and to offer support without conditions. I realized that true healing comes not from fixing others' problems but from walking alongside them on their journey.

My transformation from misery to ministry was not without its challenges. There were times when doubt and uncertainty crept in when I questioned whether I was making a difference. But in those moments, I turned to my faith for strength and guidance, trusting that God had a plan for me.

Today, I am grateful for the struggles that once consumed me. They have shaped me into who I am today and continue to fuel my passion for helping others. My ministry is not just a job or a duty but a calling that brings purpose and meaning to my life.

As I look back on my journey, I am reminded of the apostle Paul's words: "And we know that in all things God works for the good of those who love him, who have been called according to his purpose" (Romans 8:28). I am living proof of this truth, a testament to the transformative power of faith and redemption.

The Power of Silence and Empathy

In my journey, I've come to appreciate the profound impact of silence and empathy in connecting with others on a deeper level. There's a unique strength when we choose to listen rather than speak, to hold space for someone's pain without offering immediate solutions or judgments. Through these moments of quiet understanding, I've learned that sometimes, the most potent support we can offer is simply being present.

Silence allows us to hear and understand the pain and suffering of others truly. It creates a space for authentic connection and vulnerability, where people feel safe sharing their struggles without fear of judgment or criticism. In these moments, I've discovered that my presence can be a source of comfort and solace, offering a shoulder to lean on and an empathetic ear to listen.

Empathy is the ability to put ourselves in someone else's shoes and to understand and share their feelings and experiences honestly. It requires us to set aside our judgments and biases and approach others with compassion and understanding. Through practicing empathy, I've learned to see the world through a different lens and recognize the humanity in each person I encounter.

Silence and empathy form a powerful combination that can bring healing and transformation to hurting people. By listening with compassion, we create a space for healing and growth where people feel seen, heard, and valued. True healing and transformation can occur through these moments of connection.

In my own life, I've experienced the profound impact of silence and empathy in giving and receiving support. There have been times when I've felt overwhelmed by my struggles, and it's been the simple act of someone sitting with me in silence that has brought me comfort and reassurance. Similarly, I've had the privilege of offering support to others in their times of need, and I've seen firsthand the difference that a listening ear and a compassionate heart can make.

As I continue on my journey, I'm committed to cultivating a spirit of silence and empathy in my interactions with others. By practicing these qualities, I believe I can make a meaningful difference in the lives of those around me, offering hope, healing, and support to those who need it most.

Sharing the Message of Hope: Spreading the Love of Yeshua

In my faith journey, I've understood the profound love and grace that Yeshua has poured out upon me. His presence has been a source of strength and comfort, guiding me through the darkest times and leading me into the light. As I've experienced His transformative power firsthand, I've felt a deep desire to share this message of hope with others.

I recognize that not everyone may be called to stand in a pulpit and preach from the Bible, but I believe that each of us has a unique opportunity to spread the love of Yeshua in our way. Whether through acts of kindness, sharing our testimony, or simply living out our faith in our daily lives, we all have a part to play in sharing the message of hope with those around us.

For me, sharing the love of Yeshua is about more than just words; it's about living out His teachings in my interactions with others. It's about showing compassion to those in need, extending forgiveness to those who have wronged me, and offering a listening ear to those who are hurting. In these small acts of kindness and grace, I seek to reflect the love of Yeshua to the world around me.

I'm reminded of the example set by my great-great-grandfather, who served as a pastor in Panama City, FL. Though I may not have the same platform as him, I am inspired by his dedication to sharing the love of Yeshua with others. I believe that God can use me wherever I am, in whatever circumstances I find myself, to be a light in the darkness and to spread His message of hope and redemption.

As followers of Yeshua, we are called to be ambassadors of His love and grace, sharing the good news of salvation with those around us. This call is not limited to ordained ministers or missionaries; it is a call we have received as believers. By sharing the message of hope with conviction and passion, we can impact the lives of those around us and bring glory to God's name.

In sharing my journey of faith and redemption, I aim to inspire others to seek out the love and grace of Yeshua for themselves. I know firsthand the transformative power of His love and am passionate about sharing that with others. Through my words and actions, I seek to be a vessel of His love and grace, spreading hope to a world that desperately needs it.

From Relapse to Redemption: My Battle with Addiction

My battle with addiction was a relentless cycle of hope and despair, a tug-of-war between my desire for a better life and the powerful grip of substances that offered temporary escape. Each relapse felt like a failure, a step backward in a journey that I desperately wanted to move forward. I found myself in a revolving door of recovery and relapse, each time vowing it would be the last, only to find myself back in the same destructive patterns.

In the throes of addiction, the world outside seemed to blur into insignificance. The highs provided a fleeting sense of relief from the pain, but the lows dragged me deeper into the abyss. It was a suffocating existence, where each day was consumed by the need to numb my reality. The promises I made to myself and to those who cared about me were broken time and again, leading to a profound sense of shame and self-loathing.

But amidst the darkness, a glimmer of hope began to shine through. My lowest point became a turning point, a moment of clarity where I realized that I could not continue down this path. In this moment of desperation, I turned to faith, seeking strength beyond my own. I had to confront the harsh truths about my addiction, acknowledge the pain it caused, and find the courage to seek help.

The journey from relapse to redemption was far from easy. It required facing the root causes of my addiction, the unresolved pain and trauma that I had tried so hard to escape. Through therapy and counseling, I began to unpack the layers of my past, understanding the triggers that led to my substance abuse. It was a painful process, but it was also liberating. Each session peeled back a layer of hurt, revealing a stronger, more resilient version of myself.

My faith played a crucial role in my recovery. Turning to God, I found a source of unwavering support and guidance. Prayer became a lifeline, a way to connect with a higher power that gave me the strength to persevere. I learned to lean on my faith community, drawing inspiration and hope from others who had walked similar paths and emerged victorious. Their stories of redemption fueled my journey, reminding me that change was possible.

Relapse no longer signifies failure but rather a step in healing. I learned to forgive myself for the setbacks, viewing them as opportunities for growth and learning. Each relapse taught me more about my resilience and my capacity to overcome it. I began to see redemption not as a distant goal but a daily commitment to living a life of purpose and faith.

Today, my story is one of transformation. From the depths of addiction, I have risen to a place of strength and hope. My battle with addiction has become a testament to the power of faith, perseverance, and the human spirit's capacity for change. I now use my experience to help others who are struggling, offering them a message of hope and redemption. My journey from relapse to redemption reminds me that no matter how many times we fall, we have the strength to rise again and forge a new path.

Embracing Faith:
A Lifeline in Times of Crisis

Amid life's most challenging moments, faith has been my anchor, providing a lifeline that has guided me through the storm. There have been times when the weight of my struggles felt unbearable when despair threatened to swallow me whole. During these times of crisis, I discovered the profound power of embracing faith.

When I was battling addiction, it seemed like there was no end to the darkness. Every attempt to break free was met with setbacks and failures, leaving me hopeless and defeated. The turning point came when I realized I could not overcome this struggle alone. I needed something greater than myself to lean on, a source of strength and hope that could see me through the darkest hours.

Turning to God, I found the courage to face my demons head-on. Prayer became a refuge where I could pour out my fears, doubts, and pain. Through my conversations with God,

I felt a sense of peace and assurance I had never known before. It was like a heavy burden was lifted from my shoulders, replaced by a newfound hope and resilience.

Faith provided a framework for understanding my struggles. Instead of viewing my challenges as insurmountable obstacles, I began to see them as part of a more extensive journey that led me toward growth and redemption. This shift in perspective was transformative. I no longer felt like a victim of my circumstances; instead, I felt empowered to take control of my life and make meaningful changes.

My faith community also played a crucial role in my recovery during times of crisis. Surrounding myself with people who shared my beliefs and values provided an invaluable support system. They offered encouragement, understanding, and a sense of belonging that helped me navigate the difficult times. Their prayers and words of wisdom reminded me that I was not alone in my journey.

Embracing faith also taught me the importance of surrender. There were moments when the weight of my struggles was too much to bear when I felt utterly overwhelmed. In those moments, I learned to surrender my worries to God, trusting He had a plan for my life. This surrender was not about giving up but letting go of the need to control every aspect of my life and trusting in a higher power.

Through my faith, I discovered a sense of purpose that transcended my immediate struggles. I realized that my experiences, no matter how painful, had the potential to inspire and uplift others. By sharing my journey of faith and recovery, I could offer hope to those facing crises. This sense of purpose gave me the strength to keep moving forward, even when the road was difficult.

Embracing faith in times of crisis has been a transformative experience. It has given me the strength to overcome my struggles, the peace to endure difficult moments, and the hope to envision a brighter future. My faith is not just a belief system; it is a lifeline that has guided me through the darkest times and continues to be a source of strength and inspiration daily.

The Healing Power of Community Support

In my journey of recovery and transformation, one of the most profound lessons I've learned is the incredible healing power of community support. When I was at my lowest, struggling with addiction and facing the overwhelming challenges of my past, it was the support of a compassionate and understanding community that helped me find my way back to hope and healing.

Living in isolation during my darkest times only deepened my despair. The walls I built around myself to hide my pain became a prison, cutting me off from the very connections that could offer solace and strength. It wasn't until I reached out for help and allowed others into my life that I began to experience the true power of community.

The support I found in my faith community and groups like NA was life-changing. These were people who had faced their battles and emerged stronger, who understood the depths of my struggles without judgment. Their shared experiences and genuine empathy created a safe space where I could be vulnerable I could, share my story, and feel heard.

In these communities, I learned that healing is not a solitary journey. The collective strength and wisdom of the group provided a foundation upon which I could rebuild my life. Each meeting, each conversation, and each shared experience reinforced the idea that I was not alone. A network of support was ready to lift me up whenever I stumbled.

The encouragement and accountability I found within these groups were pivotal in my recovery. Knowing that others were rooting for my success and believed in my ability to overcome gave me the courage to persevere through the toughest moments. The friendships I formed were built on a foundation of trust and mutual support, and these bonds became a source of strength and resilience.

Community support also introduced me to the concept of giving back. As I progressed, I realized the importance of contributing to the community that had given me so much. I found a renewed sense of purpose by sharing my story and offering support to others who were beginning their paths to recovery. This act of giving back helped others and reinforced my commitment to healing and growth.

The healing power of community support lies in its ability to create a sense of belonging and purpose. It transforms the isolation of individual struggles into a collective journey toward wellness. Through the compassion, understanding, and encouragement of a supportive community, I discovered the strength to overcome my challenges and the resilience to build a brighter future.

Today, I continue to rely on the support of my community, and I am committed to being a source of support for others. The connections I've made have become an integral part of my life, reminding me daily of the power of human connection and the profound impact of shared experiences. My journey has taught me that no one has to face their struggles alone; a community is always ready to offer a helping hand and a compassionate heart.

A New Beginning: Finding Fulfillment in Service

When I reflect on my journey from the depths of addiction and despair to a life filled with purpose and hope, I realize that a critical turning point was finding fulfillment in service to others. My past struggles and experiences have shaped me into who I am today, and they have given me a unique perspective and a deep sense of empathy for those who are still battling their demons.

For years, I felt lost, consumed by my pain, and unable to see beyond my immediate struggles. It wasn't until I began to reach out and help others that I discovered a new sense of purpose. Service became a beacon of light in my life, guiding me out of the darkness and into a place of healing and fulfillment.

Helping others facing similar challenges has given me a profound sense of meaning. Sharing my story and offering support to those who are struggling with addiction, homelessness, or other hardships has allowed me to turn my past pain into a powerful tool for positive change. Each person I help reminds me of how far I've come and reinforces my commitment to staying on this path.

Serving others has also deepened my recovery. It keeps me grounded and focused on what truly matters. When I see the impact that my support can have on someone's life, it strengthens my resolve to continue my journey of healing. Service has become an integral part of my daily life, providing constant motivation and inspiration.

Finding fulfillment in service has also taught me the importance of community. The connections I've made through helping others have created an invaluable network of support. These relationships are built on mutual respect and understanding, providing a sense of belonging I had long missed. Together, we lift each other, celebrate our victories, and support each other through the challenges.

My journey has shown me that fulfillment doesn't come from material possessions or superficial achievements. It comes from making a difference in the lives of others and from knowing that my experiences can inspire hope and change. By dedicating myself to service, I have found a renewed sense of purpose that drives me forward.

Service has transformed my life in ways I never imagined. It has given me a new beginning, a chance to rewrite my story, and a chance to help others do the same. Each day is an opportunity to make a positive impact, offer a helping hand, and show compassion to those who need it most. Through service, I have found fulfillment and a profound sense of peace and joy that I once thought was out of reach.

"Strength isn't measured by the absence of struggle, but by the courage to face it head-on."
- Maya Angelou

As I continue this path, I am reminded that true fulfillment comes from giving back. Through service, I have found my calling, and it is through helping others that I continue to see my strength and purpose. This new beginning is not just about my recovery; it is about creating a ripple effect of hope and healing in everyone I touch.

10 MISERY INTO MINISTRY

"For we walk by faith and not by sight."
2 Corinthians 5:7

In the intricate tapestry of human existence, a profound theme exists: walking by faith, not by sight. This narrative thread, woven through the fabric of personal experience, depicts a journey of profound transformation. It begins with the raw authenticity of descent into darkness and ascends towards the illuminating dawn of redemption.

Herein lies a tale of grappling with the erosion of faith amidst the tumult of addiction and despair. The protagonist finds themselves adrift, bereft of hope, navigating a world devoid of certainty. Yet, within the crucible of adversity, a flicker of hope emerges—a recognition that surrendering to a higher power can catalyze a seismic shift in fortune.

This narrative is a testament to the resilience of the human spirit, underscored by the tenacity that arises from the depths of despair. Through trials and tribulations, amidst the labyrinthine passages of doubt, the protagonist unearths an unwavering faith—a guiding light amidst the storm of life.

This story serves as an ode to the transformative power of faith—a call to embrace the unknown, to traverse the turbulent terrain of existence with unyielding conviction. When we walk by faith, not by sight, we embark on a journey of self-discovery—a pilgrimage towards wholeness, towards realizing our truest selves.

The Power of Trusting in the Unseen

Embracing the unseen forces that weave the tapestry of my existence is akin to embarking on a profound journey of self- discovery and empowerment. It transcends the confines of the tangible world, inviting me to relinquish control and surrender to the ineffable mysteries that shape my path.

In the grand narrative of life, where uncertainty reigns supreme and challenges abound, trusting in the unseen becomes a beacon of hope amidst the darkness. It's a courageous leap into the unknown, guided by an unwavering belief in a higher purpose that transcends the limitations of human comprehension.

Trusting in the unseen is not a passive surrender but rather an active affirmation of faith—a declaration that despite the vicissitudes of fate, there exists a divine orchestration at play, intricately choreographing every twist and turn of my journey.

Faith becomes my guiding light in the labyrinthine corridors of existence, where doubts and uncertainties lurk at every corner. This steadfast companion illuminates the path ahead, even when the destination remains obscured.

It's a testament to resilience, an unwavering conviction that propels me forward, even in adversity. Through the veil of uncertainty, I glimpse the contours of a greater design—a mosaic of possibilities waiting to unfold, guided by the unseen hand of destiny.

Trusting in the unseen is a profound act of defiance—an assertion of agency in a world fraught with chaos and unpredictability. It's a testament to the human spirit's capacity to transcend the confines of the material realm and tap into the boundless reservoirs of faith that lie within.

At its essence, it recognizes the interconnectedness of all things—an acknowledgment that we are but threads in the intricate tapestry of existence, woven together by the unseen threads of fate.

In the tapestry of life, faith serves as the golden thread that binds me to the divine—a source of solace and strength in times of turmoil. It's a reminder that even in the darkest of nights, a guiding light exists—a beacon of hope that leads me ever onward toward realizing my true potential.

As I navigate the uncharted waters of existence, I do so with a sense of purpose and conviction, secure in the knowledge that I walk not alone but hand in hand with the unseen forces that guide my path.

From Despair to Redemption: A Personal Journey

In the tapestry of my life, there exists a chapter marked by profound despair, a period where hope seemed but a distant memory, and faith, a flickering ember in the darkness. This journey from despair to redemption is not just a story—it's a testament to the resilience of the human spirit and the transformative power of faith.

My descent into despair began with missteps and misfortunes that left me feeling lost and alone. Addiction tightened its grip, pulling me into a vortex of hopelessness where every day felt like a battle for survival. The vibrant colors of life faded into a monochrome existence, and I found myself questioning the very foundation of my beliefs. It was a time when the light at the end of the tunnel seemed extinguished, leaving me in a void where faith had no place.

Yet, within this abyss, a spark of determination ignited. The realization that I could not traverse this treacherous path alone became my turning point. Seeking help was a courageous step towards healing, not a sign of weakness. Rehabilitation became my sanctuary, where I began to piece together the fragments of my shattered spirit. Surrounded by those who believed in my potential, I started to pray again. Each whispered plea was a brick in the road to recovery.

This phase of my journey was one of gradual renewal. Faith, once a mere ember, began to blaze anew. My relationship with a higher power, with Yeshua, was rebuilt on the bedrock of trust and surrender. Each day brought new challenges and victories as I learned to lean on a power greater than myself. It was a period of rebuilding, where every small step forward was a triumph against the darkness that had once enveloped me.

Emerging from the shadows, I stood at the dawn of redemption. Now a steadfast guide, my faith illuminated a once impassable path. With each stride, I felt the weight of my past lifting, replaced by a profound sense of purpose and direction. Trusting in God's plan, I embraced a future where obstacles became opportunities and setbacks transformed into stepping stones.

Redemption was not just a return to faith but a complete transformation. It was a reclamation of my life, an affirmation that even the most broken can be made whole. This journey taught me that with faith, all things are possible—no matter how deep the despair, there is always a way back to the light.

"From Despair to Redemption: A Personal Journey" is more than a chronicle of my struggles; it is a beacon of hope for those in the darkest places. It is a powerful reminder that no matter how far we fall, the path to redemption is always within reach. Through faith, perseverance, and the unwavering belief in a higher power, I discovered that the journey from despair to redemption is not only possible but profoundly transformative.

Navigating Life's Challenges Through Faith

Life's a rollercoaster, full of twists and turns that can leave us feeling dizzy and disoriented. The unexpected hits us when we least expect it—personal losses, health crises, financial setbacks, relationship troubles. These challenges test our resilience, pushing us to the brink. Without a solid foundation, it's easy to get swept away by the chaos.

This is where faith steps in. Faith isn't just a comforting idea; it's an anchor that keeps us grounded amidst the storm. It's the belief that there's a higher purpose at work, no matter how rough the waters get. Faith isn't about blind hope; it's about trusting in something greater than ourselves, even when we can't see the whole picture.

Faith becomes a wellspring of strength. When life's challenges seem insurmountable, turning to prayer, meditation, and worship provides solace and clarity. These practices cultivate a sense of inner peace, a steady calm that helps us navigate the roughest seas. With faith, we're reminded that we're never truly alone. A higher power watches over us, guiding our steps and offering support when needed.

But faith does more than offer comfort—it shifts our perspective. It helps us see beyond the immediate pain and turmoil, recognizing that challenges are opportunities in disguise. They're lessons that build our character, strengthen our resolve, and deepen our spirit. Faith provides the hope that the dawn will break no matter how dark the night is. It assures us that there's light at the end of the tunnel, even if we can't see it yet.

Navigating life's challenges through faith also involves taking practical steps. It means listening to that inner voice, the divine whisper that nudges us towards the right decisions.

It's about seeking help, showing compassion to ourselves and others, and staying true to our values. Faith guides us to act with integrity and humility, even when the going gets tough.

Community plays a pivotal role in this journey. Faith often ties us to a network of like-minded individuals who offer support, encouragement, and understanding. Engaging with a faith community amplifies our resilience, reinforcing our sense of belonging and purpose. Shared beliefs and collective prayers create a powerful force that can uplift us in our darkest moments.

In essence, navigating life's challenges through faith is about embracing the journey, trusting that each step—no matter how difficult—is part of a divine plan. It's about walking with confidence and peace, knowing that a higher power is guiding us. We can face any storm with faith and become stronger on the other side.

Rebuilding Faith: Overcoming Doubt and Finding Purpose

Life's relentless ups and downs can shake even the strongest of us, making my faith and sense of purpose murky. In these moments, doubt seeps in, casting shadows over beliefs that once felt rock solid. Yet, rebuilding faith can lead to a more profound, resilient belief system and a clearer, more purposeful path forward.

Facing and Embracing Doubt

Doubt is a natural, inevitable part of the human experience. It's that persistent whisper that questions everything I thought I knew. This uncertainty often arises from personal struggles, unanswered prayers, or the sheer magnitude of suffering I witness. The first step in rebuilding faith is facing this doubt head-on rather than shoving it into a dark corner. Acknowledging doubt isn't about defeat; it's about opening the door to growth and deeper understanding.

The Journey of Overcoming Doubt

Overcoming doubt isn't about finding all the answers but learning to live harmoniously with the questions. It's a journey that demands patience, introspection, and spiritual exploration. Seeking guidance through prayer, meditation, and heartfelt conversations with trusted mentors can illuminate the path. This process might take time, but each step brings more clarity and reassurance.

Rediscovering Purpose

In doubt, my sense of purpose often feels obscured, like a distant star hidden behind clouds. Rebuilding faith means rediscovering that star and letting it guide me once more. This renewed purpose is richer and more nuanced, shaped by the trials and tribulations that spurred my quest for faith. It's a realization that my purpose and faith are deeply intertwined, reinforcing the other.

The Strength in Vulnerability

Rebuilding faith requires me to be vulnerable to admit my fears, uncertainties, and need for divine guidance. This openness leads to a more authentic and deeper connection with a higher power. In this vulnerability, I find strength, and my rebuilt faith becomes a sturdy foundation that supports me through life's storms.

Building a Resilient Faith

As I navigate through doubt and rediscover my purpose, my faith emerges stronger and more resilient. This renewed faith isn't naive; it's robust and tested, having weathered the storms of doubt. It offers a deeper sense of peace, understanding, and a profound connection to the divine.

Practical Steps for Rebuilding Faith

Engage in Regular Spiritual Practice: Consistent prayer, meditation, and study of sacred texts help anchor my faith.

Seek Community Support: Surround myself with a supportive faith community that offers encouragement and perspective.

Reflect on Past Experiences: Consider how past challenges were overcome and how faith contributed to those victories.

Stay Open to New Understandings: Be willing to explore new interpretations and insights that can enrich my faith.

Practice Gratitude: Regularly acknowledge and give thanks for the blessings in my life, reinforcing a positive and faithful outlook.

Finding Purpose Through Service

Rediscovering my purpose often comes through acts of service. By helping others and contributing to my community, I reconnect with the core principles of my faith. Service is a tangible expression of my beliefs, solidifying my purpose and making it real and impactful.

Ongoing Growth and Faith Maintenance

Rebuilding faith isn't a one-time event; it's a continuous process. It requires regular maintenance through spiritual practices and a commitment to personal growth. By staying engaged and open to learning, my faith evolves, deepens, and provides lasting purpose and fulfillment.

Walking with Confidence: Trusting in God's Guidance

Walking confidently, especially in times of uncertainty, requires a profound trust in God's guidance. This trust doesn't come from blind faith but from a deep, personal relationship with the divine, built through prayer, reflection, and experience. Trusting in God's guidance transforms how I approach life's challenges, decisions, and everyday moments, allowing me to navigate with assurance and peace.

Divine guidance is about believing that God has a unique plan for me, crafted with love and purpose. This plan may only be clear sometimes, and it often unfolds unexpectedly. Trusting in this guidance means accepting that I won't always have all the answers or see the whole picture, but I can move forward with confidence, knowing that God is leading the way.

God's guidance often comes in subtle nudges rather than grand revelations. It might be a gentle push to take a new direction, an unexpected opportunity that aligns with my inner values, or a whisper of reassurance during tough times.

Recognizing these divine nudges requires a tuned spiritual ear developed through consistent prayer and mindfulness. These small, everyday moments of guidance build my confidence in God's presence and plan.

Prayer is my lifeline to God's guidance. I find clarity and direction in these quiet moments of communion. By dedicating daily time to prayer and reflection, I open my heart to receive God's wisdom. Journaling my thoughts and prayers helps me track guidance patterns over time, reinforcing my trust and confidence in God's ongoing presence.

Life is full of uncertainties, and it's easy to feel overwhelmed by the unknown. However, trusting in God's guidance provides a steadying force. It's like having a divine compass that reassures me I'm on the right path, even when the way forward seems unclear. This trust allows me to confidently step into the unknown, knowing I'm not walking alone.

Reflecting on past experiences where God's guidance was evident strengthens my faith. These moments, where challenges were met with unexpected solutions or when I felt an inexplicable peace amidst chaos, remind me of God's faithful presence. Each recollection reinforces my confidence in God's guidance, encouraging me to trust more deeply with each new step.

Being part of a faith community enhances my confidence in God's guidance. Sharing my experiences and hearing others' stories of divine direction provides mutual encouragement. This collective wisdom and support create a network of trust that bolsters my faith journey. I remind myself and others of God's unfailing guidance, especially during challenging times.

Trusting in God's guidance also means being willing to act. Hearing God's direction is not enough; I must step out in faith and follow through. This action might involve taking risks, making sacrifices, or stepping outside my comfort zone. Each act of obedience, however small, builds my confidence in God's leading and reinforces my trust.

When I trust God's guidance, I live with purpose and assurance that transcends circumstances. This confidence radiates in my decisions, relationships, and daily interactions. It's a quiet strength that others can see, a testament to the peace and direction that comes from a life guided by faith.

Walking with confidence is an ongoing journey of growth. It involves continually seeking God's guidance, learning from each experience, and deepening my trust. It's a dynamic process where faith and action intertwine, leading me toward a life that is both purposeful and fulfilled.

Faith in Action: Obedience and Steadfastness

Living out faith isn't just about believing; it's about doing. It's about putting those beliefs into action through obedience and steadfastness. When I think about faith in action, I'm reminded that true faith demands a commitment to follow God's will and remain firm in my beliefs, even when the road gets rocky.

Obedience is the cornerstone of faith in action. It's about trusting God's plan and being willing to follow His guidance, even when it doesn't align with my desires or understanding. This obedience demands humility and a willingness to surrender control, acknowledging that God's wisdom surpasses mine. In practical terms, obedience might mean making difficult choices that honor God, resisting temptations, or stepping out in faith when called to serve others.

On the other hand, Steadfastness is the unwavering commitment to my faith, regardless of circumstances. It's about holding fast to my beliefs and maintaining my integrity, even when it gets tough. Steadfastness is not just about enduring hardships but also about consistently living out my faith day by day. This persistence builds spiritual resilience and demonstrates the strength of my conviction.

One of the most profound ways I can express obedience and steadfastness is through my daily actions. It's the small, everyday decisions that reflect my commitment to God. Whether showing kindness to others, maintaining honesty in my dealings, or dedicating time to prayer and study, these actions are the building blocks of a faithful life. Each choice, no matter how minor it seems, is an opportunity to align my life with my faith.

Another critical aspect of obedience is listening to God's voice. This requires regular prayer and reflection to understand His will for my life. It means being open to the Holy Spirit's leading and being willing to act on it. Sometimes, God's call may lead me out of my comfort zone, challenging me to grow and serve in new ways. Embracing these moments with a heart of obedience can lead to profound spiritual growth and fulfillment.

Steadfastness is particularly vital when facing trials and temptations. It's easy to stay faithful when life is smooth, but true steadfastness shines through in adversity. Maintaining my faith becomes a testament to its strength when I encounter difficulties, whether personal struggles, doubts, or external pressures. In these moments of testing, my faith is refined and deepened.

Community plays a significant role in fostering obedience and steadfastness. Surrounding myself with fellow believers who share my commitment to living out faith provides support and encouragement. We can hold each other accountable, pray for one another, and share the journey of faith. This communal aspect of faith helps reinforce my resolve and keeps me grounded.

Reflecting on the lives of biblical figures who exemplified obedience and steadfastness can inspire and guide me. Stories of people like Abraham, who obeyed God's call without knowing where it would lead, or Daniel, who remained steadfast in his faith despite facing a lion's den, offer powerful examples of faith in action. Their experiences remind me that my faith journey is part of a much larger narrative of God's work throughout history.

Ultimately, faith in action through obedience and steadfastness is about trusting in God's promises and holding onto hope. It's about believing God is faithful, even when I can't see the way forward. This trust empowers me to act with courage and perseverance, knowing that my faith is grounded in God's unchanging character.

By embracing obedience and steadfastness, I can live out my faith in a way that honors God, transforms my life, and impacts those around me. It's a continual growth and commitment journey that leads to a deeper, more vibrant relationship with God.

Living Out Faith:
Putting Beliefs into Practice

Living out faith isn't just about what I believe; it's about how I live my life. It's about taking those convictions, those deep-down beliefs, and letting them guide my every action. It's about being more than just a believer in theory—it's about being a believer in action.

For me, putting faith into practice starts with a solid foundation. It's about knowing what I believe and why I believe it. This isn't just about reciting creeds or doctrines; it's about having a personal relationship with God and understanding His teachings. It's about letting those beliefs shape who I am and how I interact with the world.

One of the most important ways I live out my faith is by serving others. This means going beyond myself and my needs and desires and reaching out to help those in need. Whether volunteering at a local soup kitchen, lending a hand to a neighbor, or simply being there for a friend in a tough time, these acts of service are tangible expressions of God's love.

Integrity is also a big part of living out faith. It's about being honest and true, even when difficult or inconvenient. It's about being the same person in private as in public, letting my actions speak louder than my words. This kind of integrity isn't always easy, but it's essential if I want my faith to have any real impact on the world around me.

Living out faith means bringing my beliefs into every aspect of my life. It's about seeking God's guidance in my decisions, big and small, and trusting He will lead me in the right direction. It's about being intentional about my relationships, work, finances—everything. It's about living with purpose and passion, knowing that every choice I make is an opportunity to glorify God.

Community is another important part of living out faith. Surrounding myself with other believers provides support, encouragement, and accountability. We can spur each other on to love and good deeds, sharing our struggles and victories. Engaging in community activities, like church groups or service projects, helps me put my faith into practice in real, tangible ways.

Living out faith also means standing up for what's right, even when it's difficult or unpopular. It's about speaking out against injustice, advocating for the marginalized, and working to improve the world. It's about being a voice for the voiceless and a champion for those who can't speak for themselves.

But most importantly, living out faith requires perseverance. It's about staying faithful even when the going gets tough, trusting that God is with me every step of the way. It's about holding onto hope, even in the darkest times, knowing that God is working all things together for my good.

Ultimately, living out faith is about more than just believing the right things—it's about letting those beliefs transform me from the inside out. It's about being a light in a dark world, a beacon of hope and love to those around me. Through my words and actions, I can show the world what it truly means to live out faith.

Embracing Hope:

Blessings of Walking by Faith

In the intricate tapestry of life, there's a thread that holds steadfast through every twist and turn: hope. But not just any hope—hope intertwined with faith, a beacon that illuminates even the darkest paths. In exploring the essence of "Embracing Hope: Blessings of Walking by Faith," we embark on a journey into the heart of belief and the richness it brings to our lives.

This heading speaks to the profound connection between faith and hope and how they intertwine to shape our perspectives and experiences. It's about more than mere optimism; it's a deep-seated assurance that regardless of what unfolds before us, there's a divine plan at work—a plan infused with hope and guided by faith.

Embracing hope within faith isn't just wishful thinking; it's a conscious choice to trust in something greater than ourselves. It's about recognizing that amidst life's trials and tribulations, there's a source of unwavering strength and comfort to be found. Through faith, we open ourselves to a cascade of blessings, each a testament to the transformative power of walking by faith.

The blessings of walking by faith are manifold, touching every facet of our existence. From the inner peace that surpasses understanding to the inexplicable joy that fills our hearts, faith infuses our lives with a sense of purpose and meaning. In those moments of surrender, when we relinquish control and place our trust in a higher power, we truly experience the blessings of walking by faith.

But the greatest blessing is the deepened relationship with the divine that faith affords us. In the quiet moments of prayer, the whispered conversations with our Creator, we find solace and strength. Through faith, we understand that we are never alone and that a guiding hand is leading us through every trial and triumph.

"Embracing Hope: Blessings of Walking by Faith" is an invitation to surrender to the journey, trust in the unseen, and embrace the boundless blessings that await us. It reminds us that even in the darkest of times, there is hope and that hope is the very essence of faith. So, let us walk boldly into the unknown, secure in the knowledge that we are guided by faith and buoyed by hope.

Nurturing Faith:
Cultivating a Vibrant Spiritual Life

As I delve into the essence of "Nurturing Faith: Cultivating a Vibrant Spiritual Life," I embark on personal introspection and growth. It's not just about maintaining faith—it's about actively tending to it, nurturing it like a precious seedling in the garden of my soul.

Cultivating a vibrant spiritual life begins with intentionality. I deliberately choose to prioritize my relationship with the divine, carving out time and space in my daily routine for prayer, meditation, and reflection. Through these practices, I water the roots of my faith, allowing them to delve deeper into the rich soil of spiritual nourishment.

Nurturing faith also involves seeking out sources of inspiration and wisdom. Whether through scripture, sacred texts, or the teachings of spiritual mentors, I continually feed my soul with the nourishment it craves. I immerse myself in the timeless truths that have sustained believers for centuries, drawing strength and guidance from their wisdom.

But nurturing faith isn't just a solitary pursuit—it's also about fostering community and connection. I seek out fellow travelers on the spiritual journey, engaging in meaningful conversations and shared faith experiences. Together, we support and uplift one another, providing encouragement and accountability.

As I tend to my faith with care and diligence, I see it flourish and bloom. I feel a deep sense of peace and contentment, knowing I am rooted in something greater than myself. My spiritual life becomes a vibrant tapestry of experiences woven together by moments of connection, revelation, and transformation.

In nurturing my faith, I also cultivate a deeper awareness of the divine presence in every aspect of my life. I begin to see God's hand at work in the ordinary moments, guiding and shaping my journey in ways I never imagined possible. My faith becomes a living, breathing reality that infuses every moment with purpose and meaning.

Ultimately, "Nurturing Faith: Cultivating a Vibrant Spiritual Life" is a call to action—a reminder that faith is not something to be taken for granted but rather something to be tended to with care and intentionality. It's an invitation to deepen my relationship with the divine to cultivate a spiritual life that is rich, vibrant, and overflowing with the blessings of faith.

Embracing Transformation: Journeying Towards Spiritual Growth

"Embracing Transformation: Journeying Towards Spiritual Growth" encapsulates the essence of my ongoing spiritual journey—a voyage marked by evolution, discovery, and profound change. It's not merely about staying stagnant in my beliefs but rather about embracing the dynamic process of growth and transformation.

As I reflect on this heading, I am reminded that spiritual growth is not a destination but a continual journey that unfolds with each step I take and each experience I encounter. It's about being open to change, new perspectives, and the transformative power of divine grace.

Embracing transformation begins with a willingness to embrace discomfort and uncertainty. It's about stepping outside my comfort zone, confronting my fears, and embracing the unknown with courage and faith. In these moments of vulnerability, actual growth occurs as I allow myself to be shaped and molded by the hands of the divine.

Journeying towards spiritual growth also involves a deep commitment to self-reflection and introspection. It's about looking inward and examining my beliefs, values, and actions honestly and humbly. Through this process of self-discovery, I uncover areas needing healing and transformation, allowing God's grace to work in me and through me.

But perhaps the most profound aspect of embracing transformation is surrender—letting go of my agenda and trusting in the divine plan for my life. It's about releasing control and allowing God to lead me where He will, even if it means walking through valleys of darkness or uncertainty. In surrendering to the journey, I find a sense of freedom and liberation—a freedom to be who I am meant to be and become all God has called me to become.

As I embrace transformation, I am reminded that growth is not always easy or comfortable. There will be challenges and obstacles, moments of doubt and fear. But in these moments, I am reminded of the transformative power of faith—the belief that God is at work in every circumstance, shaping me and molding me into His image.

Ultimately, "Embracing Transformation: Journeying Towards Spiritual Growth" is a testament to the beauty and complexity of the spiritual journey. It's an invitation to embrace change, lean into discomfort, and trust in the process of transformation. As I journey forward, I do so with an open heart and steadfast faith, knowing that God is with me every step of the way.

11 WHO BUT YOU?

"You cannot control what happens to you, but you can control your attitude toward what happens to you, and in that, you will be mastering change rather than allowing it to master you." ~ Brian Tracy

In the rollercoaster of life, responsibility isn't just a buzzword; it's the real deal that keeps me on track. It's about taking the reins of my destiny, steering through the twists and turns with determination and grit. Whether it's facing setbacks or chasing dreams, owning up to my choices is the name of the game. Responsibility isn't always easy, but it's the backbone of my hustle, pushing me to step up and own my journey.

When it comes to getting stuff done, accountability is my ride-or-die. It's about being honest with myself, setting goals, and hustling hard to make them happen. Whether grinding through tough times or celebrating wins, being accountable keeps me focused and hungry for success. It's about staying true to my word, even when the going gets tough and hustling like there's no tomorrow.

But hustling solo isn't the only way to roll; trusting in myself and my faith adds extra fuel to my hustle. It's about believing in my abilities, leaning on my intuition, and knowing I have what it takes to overcome any obstacle. Whether facing self- doubt or navigating uncharted territory, trust in myself and a higher power strengthens me to keep pushing forward. It's about staying grounded, humble, and trusting that the hustle will pay off.

Responsibility, accountability, and trust form the ultimate trifecta in my hustle game. It's about owning my journey, hustling hard, and trusting everything will fall into place. With each step forward, I'm reminded that my destiny is in my hands, and it's up to me to hustle hard and make it happen.

The Power of Taking Responsibility

In the tapestry of life, woven with joy and sorrow, triumphs and tribulations, one undeniable truth emerges – the power of taking responsibility. Through the corridors of time, I've traversed paths laden with challenges and obstacles, each a crucible for personal growth and self-discovery. It's amidst these crucibles that I've come to appreciate the profound impact of assuming ownership of my actions and decisions.

From the earliest whispers of consciousness to the present moment, I've grappled with the dichotomy of blame and accountability. In moments of failure or setback, it's tempting to cast blame upon external forces – fate, circumstance, or the actions of others. Yet, as I've journeyed through the labyrinth of existence, I've realized that the locus of control resides within – within the depths of my being, my choices, my agency.

Each twist and turn, each crossroad encountered along the way, has been a testament to the transformative power of responsibility. It's easy to relinquish agency and surrender to the currents of fate. Still, the deception lies therein, for it is by assuming responsibility and acknowledging my role in shaping my destiny that true liberation is found.

The realization dawns like the first light – I am the master of my fate, the architect of my destiny. With the mantle of responsibility draped upon my shoulders, I stand poised to chart a course through the tumultuous seas of life. It is a journey fraught with uncertainty yet imbued with boundless potential.

Each step forward reminds me of the sacred covenant between action and consequence. Every choice made, every path chosen, leaves an indelible mark upon the fabric of existence. I forge my identity, legacy, and essence through the crucible of responsibility.

In embracing responsibility, I embrace life itself—in all its complexity, beauty, and chaos. Through the crucible of responsibility, I discover the true essence of freedom—the freedom to shape my destiny, carve my path, and transcend the limitations of circumstance.

So, as I stand upon the threshold of tomorrow, I do so with a newfound sense of purpose and resolve. In the crucible of responsibility lies the promise of transformation, the genesis of a life lived with intention and meaning. It is a journey fraught with challenges yet illuminated by the radiant light of self- discovery and personal growth.

The power of taking responsibility is not merely a choice – it is a sacred duty, a solemn vow to honor the sanctity of life itself. And so, with each passing moment, I embrace this mantle with open arms, knowing that therein lies the key to unlocking the boundless potential that resides within.

Mastering Change Through Accountability

As I navigate the labyrinth of life's uncertainties and confront the ever-shifting landscape of change, I am reminded of accountability's pivotal role in mastering the tumultuous tides of existence. Like an unrelenting storm, change sweeps through the corridors of time, leaving a trail of upheaval and transformation in its wake. Yet, amidst the chaos, it is not the force of change that determines one's fate but how one chooses to respond.

In embracing the mantle of accountability, I recognize that I am not merely a passive bystander in the face of change but an active participant in shaping its course. This realization dawns with the clarity of revelation—that while I may not have control over the external forces that buffet my life, I possess agency over my response.

Accountability, in its essence, is a beacon of light amidst the storm, guiding me through the murky depths of uncertainty with clarity and purpose. It is the recognition that, in every moment of challenge or adversity lies an opportunity for growth and self-discovery. By owning my actions and decisions, I transform change from a precursor of fear and anxiety into a catalyst for personal evolution.

In the crucible of accountability, I am empowered to transcend the limitations of circumstance, rise above the tumultuous currents of fate, and chart a course toward a brighter tomorrow. This journey is fraught with challenges and obstacles yet imbued with boundless potential and opportunity.

As I stand upon the precipice of transformation, I am reminded that true mastery of change lies not in resistance but in acceptance. It is the willingness to embrace the unknown, relinquish the illusion of control, and surrender to the ebb and flow of life's ever-changing rhythms.

In the crucible of accountability, I discovered the true essence of resilience—the ability to adapt and thrive amidst the shifting sands of time. This is a testament to the indomitable spirit of the human soul, capable of weathering any storm and emerging more substantial on the other side.

So, as I journey through the ever-changing landscape of existence, I do so with a newfound sense of clarity and purpose. For in the crucible of accountability lies the key to mastering change, the promise of a life lived with intention and meaning. And so, with each passing moment, I embrace the challenges that lie ahead, knowing that therein lies the opportunity for growth, transformation, and personal evolution.

The Ultimate Responsibility: Shaping Your Destiny

As I embark on self-discovery and personal growth, I am acutely aware of the importance of assuming responsibility for shaping my destiny. In the grand tapestry of existence, each thread of my life is woven with my choices, actions, and paths I choose to traverse. Within the crucible of responsibility, I discover the true extent of my agency – the power to sculpt my fate, to carve out a future that reflects my deepest aspirations and desires.

The Power of Self-Determination

In embracing the mantle of responsibility, I recognize that I am the master of my destiny. This realization dawns with the clarity of revelation—that while external forces may buffet my life, I alone possess the agency to chart the course of my journey. It is a journey fraught with uncertainty and challenge yet imbued with boundless potential and opportunity.

Navigating Life's Crossroads

At every juncture of life, I am confronted with choices that shape the trajectory of my existence and determine the path I ultimately tread. Within the crucible of responsibility, I find the courage to confront these crossroads head-on, weigh the pros and cons, and make decisions that align with my values and aspirations. In doing so, I lay the foundation for a future imbued with purpose, passion, and fulfillment.

The Role of Faith and Guidance

In navigating the complexities of life's journey, I am guided by the unwavering support and divine guidance bestowed upon me. Through the lens of faith, I find solace amidst the storms of uncertainty, trusting in a higher power to illuminate the path ahead. With each step forward, I am reminded of the sacred covenant between action and consequence, knowing that my choices reverberate through the corridors of time, shaping the tapestry of my destiny.

Embracing Change with Grace

Change, like a relentless tide, sweeps through the landscape of my existence, reshaping the contours of my reality with each passing moment. Within the crucible of responsibility, I find the strength to embrace change with grace and resilience and adapt and evolve amidst life's evershifting currents. This is a testament to the indomitable spirit of the human soul, capable of weathering any storm and emerging more substantial on the other side.

The Promise of Personal Fulfillment

In assuming responsibility for shaping my destiny, I unlock the promise of personal fulfillment – realizing my deepest aspirations and desires. It is a journey fraught with challenges and obstacles, yet illuminated by the radiant light of self- discovery and growth. With each passing moment, I am reminded of the sacred covenant between action and consequence, knowing that my choices shape the tapestry of my destiny and pave the way for a future imbued with purpose and meaning.

So, as I journey through the labyrinth of existence, I do so with a newfound sense of purpose and resolve. For in the crucible of responsibility lies the promise of a life lived with intention and meaning – a life sculpted by my hands, guided by faith, and driven by the unwavering resolve to embrace the journey with open arms.

Navigating Life's Choices: Embracing Change with Grace

In the tapestry of my existence, change emerges as an immutable force, reshaping the contours of my reality with each passing moment.

As I navigate the labyrinth of life, I am confronted with the inevitability of change. This relentless tide sweeps through the corridors of time, leaving a trail of transformation and evolution.

Within the crucible of responsibility, I find the strength to embrace change with grace and resilience, navigating life's ever-shifting landscape with courage and determination.

Change is an inherent aspect of life, like the tides' ebb and flow. It manifests in myriad forms—from the subtle shifts of seasons to the seismic upheavals of personal transformation. Rather than resisting change, I embrace it as an opportunity for growth and self-discovery.

In the face of change, I remain steadfast and resilient, adapting to life's ever-shifting landscape with courage and determination. Like a tree bending with the wind, I flex and yield to the currents of change, knowing that resilience lies in my ability to adapt and evolve.

Change often heralds the unknown – a realm fraught with uncertainty and possibility. Rather than succumbing to fear or doubt, I embrace the unknown with open arms, trusting in the journey and its lessons.

In moments of upheaval and uncertainty, I draw upon my wellspring of resilience, finding strength in adversity and courage in the face of uncertainty. Through the crucible of change, I discover the depth of my resilience—an indomitable spirit capable of weathering any storm.

Transitions, though fraught with challenges, are also ripe with opportunity. With each transition, I navigate the unknown with grace and poise, trusting in my ability to adapt and thrive amidst the changing currents of life.

As I roll through life's crazy rollercoaster, I do it with a sense of purpose and a 'bring it on' attitude. In the heat of it all lies the promise of transformation—a journey of selfdiscovery and growth guided by my unshakeable resolve to embrace change with swagger and resilience.

Fulfilling My Destiny: The Promise of Personal Growth

As I traverse the winding roads of life, I am keenly aware of the profound significance of fulfilling my destiny. It's not merely about wandering through the corridors of existence but about embracing my unique journey with purpose and intention. Within the realm of responsibility lies the promise of personal growth – a journey marked by self-discovery, resilience, and the fulfillment of my deepest aspirations.

Embracing My Unique Journey:

In embracing the mantle of responsibility, I acknowledge that my journey is mine alone. I realize that each twist and turn, each triumph and setback, contributes to the tapestry of my existence. Rather than comparing my path to others or seeking validation from external sources, I embrace the uniqueness of my journey with gratitude and humility.

Unveiling Layers of Self-Discovery:

Along the path of responsibility lies the profound journey of self-discovery. It's a journey marked by introspection, self- awareness, and the unraveling of layers that define my essence. Through moments of reflection and contemplation,

I peel back the layers of conditioning and societal expectations to uncover the authentic self that resides within me.

Cultivating Resilience Amidst Adversity:

Adversity, though formidable, serves as a crucible for personal growth and resilience. Within the crucible of responsibility, I discover the depth of my inner strength – the resilience to weather life's storms and emerge stronger on the other side. I lean into the discomfort with each challenge, knowing that growth lies on the other side of adversity.

Pursuing Deepest Aspirations:

Fulfilling my destiny entails aligning my actions with my deepest aspirations and desires. I set bold intentions, chase my dreams with unwavering determination, and refuse to settle for anything less than what sets my soul on fire. With each step I take *toward my goals, I move closer to fulfilling my destiny.*

Finding Meaning and Purpose:

Ultimately, fulfilling my destiny is imbued with meaning and purpose. It's about contributing my unique gifts and talents to the world, positively impacting, and leaving a legacy that transcends my time. As I embrace responsibility and chart my course with intention, I uncover the profound meaning of my existence.

As I fulfill my destiny, I do so with anticipation and excitement. For in the crucible of responsibility lies the promise of personal growth, fulfillment, and realizing my deepest aspiration.

The Power of Accountability in Achieving My Goals

In my pursuit of personal growth and fulfillment, I understand the profound power of accountability. Holding myself accountable for my actions and decisions is a cornerstone of my journey toward achieving my goals and dreams. Through accountability, I find the focus, motivation, and resilience needed to navigate the challenges and triumphs along my path.

Accountability is not merely a concept but a practice that I integrate into every aspect of my life. It begins with setting clear, measurable goals that align with my values and aspirations. These goals serve as the compass guiding my actions, ensuring that every step I take moves me closer to realizing my dreams.

Setting Clear, Measurable Goals

The first step in embracing accountability is to set clear and measurable goals. This involves defining what I want to achieve and breaking it into actionable steps. By establishing specific, realistic targets, I create a roadmap that directs my efforts and keeps me focused on my objectives.

Staying Focused and Motivated

Accountability serves as a powerful motivator. When I hold myself accountable, I remain committed to my goals, even when faced with obstacles or setbacks. This commitment drives me to stay focused and motivated, pushing through challenges with determination and resilience. It reminds me that my success is directly tied to my actions and decisions.

Overcoming Obstacles with Resilience

Life is filled with obstacles and unexpected challenges. Accountability equips me with the resilience needed to overcome these hurdles. By taking ownership of my choices, I empower myself to find solutions and adapt to changing circumstances. Each challenge becomes an opportunity to learn, grow, and strengthen my resolve.

Reflecting on Progress

A critical aspect of accountability is regular reflection on my progress. This involves assessing my achievements, identifying improvement areas, and celebrating my successes. Reflecting on my journey allows me to adjust my strategies, stay aligned with my goals, and maintain a sense of accomplishment.

Seeking Support and Guidance

While accountability begins with me, seeking support and guidance from others can enhance my efforts. By sharing my goals with trusted mentors, friends, or accountability partners, I create a network of support that encourages and holds me accountable. These relationships provide valuable feedback, encouragement, and perspective, enriching my journey.

Embracing Continuous Improvement

Accountability is not a one-time act but a continuous process of improvement. It requires me to be honest, acknowledge my mistakes, and commit to learning and growing. By embracing continuous improvement, I ensure that I am always moving forward, refining my approach, and striving to be the best version of myself.

By embracing the power of accountability, I unlock my potential to achieve my goals and dreams. Through this practice, I find the focus, motivation, and resilience to navigate my journey with purpose and determination. By holding myself accountable, I take control of my destiny, creating a life that is fulfilling, meaningful, and aligned with my deepest aspirations.

Trusting in Myself and My Faith

Navigating the complexities of life has taught me one crucial lesson: the importance of trusting in myself and my faith. This trust is a foundation upon which I build my resilience, shape my decisions, and find my direction amidst the chaos. It's about forging a strong sense of self-reliance while seeking guidance from a higher power.

Cultivating Self-Reliance

Trusting in myself begins with cultivating self-reliance. It's the realization that I am the primary architect of my life. This doesn't mean I'm alone in my journey, but it underscores the necessity of taking responsibility for my actions and decisions.

I've learned to listen to my inner voice and value my instincts and judgment. I use my experiences and inner strength to navigate a challenge when faced with it. This self-reliance empowers me, providing the confidence to face life's uncertainties.

Leaning on Faith

While self-reliance is essential, leaning on my faith is equally important. My belief in a higher power provides comfort and direction, especially during difficult times. Trusting in God helps me understand that I am part of a larger plan, one that is guided by divine wisdom and love.

This faith reassures me that work has a greater purpose, even when things don't go according to my plans. It gives me the strength to surrender control, knowing that I am supported and guided by a force greater than myself.

Balancing Independence and Faith

Balancing self-reliance with faith involves understanding that while I am responsible for my actions, I am also supported by a higher power. This balance provides a sense of harmony, where I take initiative and make decisions but remain open to divine guidance and intervention.

Trusting in myself means setting goals and working diligently towards them, while trusting in my faith means believing that I am never truly alone in my efforts. This dual trust forms the backbone of my resilience and perseverance.

Overcoming Self-Doubt

One of the biggest obstacles in life is self-doubt. There are moments when my confidence wavers and uncertainty clouds my vision. In these times, trusting myself and my faith becomes even more critical.

I remind myself of past successes and lessons learned from failures to overcome self-doubt. I draw strength from my faith, believing that every challenge is an opportunity for growth and that I am equipped to handle whatever comes my way.

Embracing Life's Challenges

Life's challenges are inevitable, but trusting in myself and my faith helps me embrace them with courage and grace. This trust allows me to view obstacles not as insurmountable barriers but as stepping stones toward personal growth and fulfillment.

With each challenge, I learn more about my capabilities and the power of my faith. This continuous journey of overcoming and learning reinforces my belief in myself and deepens my faith.

Finding Peace and Fulfillment

Ultimately, trusting in myself and my faith leads to a profound sense of peace and fulfillment. It allows me to navigate life purposefully, knowing I am capable and supported. This trust gives me the confidence to pursue my dreams, face my fears, and live authentically.

In trusting myself, I honor my potential and my unique path. In trusting my faith, I acknowledge the divine presence that guides and sustains me. Together, these elements create a foundation of strength and resilience that empowers me to live a fulfilling and meaningful life.

Through this journey of trust, I discovered that life's challenges and uncertainties are not to be feared but embraced. In these moments, I truly learned to trust in my strength and the faith surrounding me.

Cultivating Creativity: Embracing Innovation and Inspiration

In my journey through life, I've realized the profound importance of cultivating creativity. It's not just about artistic expression or thinking outside the box; it's about tapping into the boundless well of innovation and inspiration within each of us. Creativity isn't just a skill; it's a way of life—a mindset that shapes how I approach challenges, solve problems, and navigate the world around me.

Embracing creativity means embracing the unknown and venturing into uncharted territory with curiosity and courage. It's about breaking free from the constraints of convention and embracing the freedom to explore new ideas, perspectives, and possibilities. Whether brainstorming new solutions, pursuing a passion project, or simply daydreaming, I strive to foster an environment that nurtures and celebrates creativity in all its forms.

At its core, creativity is about connection—connecting dots, connecting ideas, and connecting people. It's about finding patterns in chaos, making sense of the nonsensical, and forging meaningful connections that spark innovation and collaboration. By embracing creativity, I unlock my potential and contribute to a larger ecosystem of innovation and inspiration, where ideas flow freely and boundaries blur.

Cultivating creativity is more important than ever in a constantly evolving world. It's about embracing uncertainty, failure, and the messy, beautiful process of creation. By nurturing my imagination, I enrich my life and contribute to a brighter, more innovative future.

Environmental Consciousness: Nurturing Our Planet for Future Generations

In my journey toward environmental consciousness, I've realized the urgent need to nurture our planet for the well-being of future generations. It's not merely about individual actions but a collective responsibility to safeguard the Earth's precious resources and protect its delicate ecosystems. As I navigate through life, I am constantly reminded of the interconnectedness between humanity and the environment and our actions' profound impact on the world around us.

Nurturing our planet begins with a deep respect and appreciation for the natural world. It's about recognizing the inherent value of biodiversity, the beauty of untouched landscapes, and the delicate balance that sustains life on Earth. From the majestic mountains to the vast oceans, every corner of our planet is teeming with life, and it's our responsibility to preserve and protect it for future generations.

As I strive to live more sustainably, I am mindful of my choices and their environmental impact. Whether it's reducing my carbon footprint, conserving water, or minimizing waste, every action I take is a step towards a more sustainable future. From adopting eco-friendly habits in my daily life to advocating for policy changes on a larger scale, I am committed to being a steward of the Earth and leaving behind a legacy of environmental stewardship.

But environmental consciousness goes beyond individual actions; it's about fostering a culture of sustainability in our communities and societies. It's about coming together to address global challenges like climate change, deforestation, and pollution and working towards solutions that benefit both people and the planet. By raising awareness, inspiring action, and promoting environmental literacy, we can create a world where future generations can thrive in harmony with nature.

In the end, nurturing our planet is not just a responsibility— it's a moral imperative. It's about recognizing our interconnectedness with the Earth and taking meaningful action to protect and preserve it for future generations. As I continue my journey toward environmental consciousness, I am inspired by the hope that together, we can create a more sustainable and resilient world for all.

Digital Wellness:
Striking a Balance in the Digital Age

In my exploration of digital wellness, I recognize the importance of finding balance in an increasingly digital world. It's not just about staying connected or being productive; it's about fostering a healthy relationship with technology that enhances rather than detracts from my wellbeing. As I navigate through the digital landscape, I am constantly mindful of the impact of my digital habits on my mental, emotional, and physical health.

Striking a balance in the digital age begins with mindfulness—a conscious awareness of how I engage with technology and its effects on my life. It's about being intentional with my screen time, setting boundaries, and taking regular breaks to recharge and refocus. Whether it's limiting social media use, practicing digital detoxes, or prioritizing real- life interactions, I strive to cultivate a healthy relationship with technology that serves me rather than controls me.

At the heart of digital wellness lies the need for self-care and self-compassion. It's about recognizing when I need to disconnect and prioritize my well-being over the constant demands of the digital world. From practicing mindfulness meditation to engaging in offline hobbies and activities, I prioritize activities that nourish my mind, body, and soul, allowing me to find balance amidst the digital noise.

But digital wellness is not just an individual endeavor; it's also about creating environments and communities that support healthy digital habits. It's about fostering open conversations about the impact of technology on our lives, advocating for policies that promote digital well-being, and building platforms that prioritize user safety and mental health. By coming together to address the challenges of the digital age, we can create a more inclusive and compassionate online world for all.

12 A NEW YOU

"Though no one can go back and make a brand new start, anyone can start from now and make a brand new ending." ~Carl Bard

Embracing my authentic self is the first step toward true happiness and fulfillment. From a young age, I learned to seek approval and acceptance from others, often changing who I was to fit in. However, absolute acceptance comes from within. By loving and accepting myself, flaws and all, I can live a life of integrity, joy, and purpose. Standing alone and being true to myself is a sign of strength, allowing me to celebrate my uniqueness and individuality.

My transformation began with the understanding that my past no longer defines me. As a born-again believer, I have been given a new beginning in Yeshua, washing away my past mistakes and sins. This spiritual renewal has freed me from the bondage of my previous life, enabling me to embrace my new identity and step into the fullness of who God has created me to be. Each day is an opportunity to start fresh, leaving behind old habits and patterns that no longer serve me.

Trusting in God's plan is crucial for finding true fulfillment and purpose in life. God's timing is perfect, and His ways are higher than mine. I can find peace and assurance by letting go of my need to control and understanding that He is guiding my steps. Embracing the new opportunities and paths He presents requires courage, but it leads to growth and transformation. Knowing God is in control allows me to pursue my dreams and live meaningfully.

Walking in freedom and abundance means trusting God's provision and His promises. This encompasses all aspects of life, from material wealth to peace, joy, and purpose. With my rebirth in Yeshua, I have the power to overcome past strongholds and live a life of integrity. Celebrating new beginnings and embracing the opportunities God provides allows me to walk confidently into the future He has prepared. I can live an abundant and fulfilling life by trusting God's plan and love.

Embracing Your Authentic Self

I often find myself trying to fit in and be accepted by others. The temptation to follow the crowd is strong, even when I know deep down that I am meant to stand alone.

The truth is, I can never indeed be happy or fulfilled if I am not being true to myself. God has a unique plan for us, and I must embrace my authentic self and live out that plan.

From a young age, I was taught to seek approval and acceptance from others. I changed my behavior, beliefs, and appearance to fit in and be liked by those around me.

However, true acceptance comes from within. I must learn to love and accept myself for who I am and my flaws. I can only find peace and contentment by recognizing my worth and valuing my individuality.

It is easy to get caught up in the crowd mentality, going along with the majority even when it goes against my beliefs or values. But standing alone and being true to myself is a sign of strength, not weakness.

It takes courage to be different, to stand out, and to follow my path, even if it means going against the grain. This strength comes from within and is a testament to my authenticity.

True happiness and fulfillment lie in embracing my authentic self, letting go of the need to be something I am not, and celebrating my uniqueness and individuality.

Being true to myself can help me live a life of integrity, joy, and purpose. It's about aligning my actions and decisions with my true nature and beliefs rather than conforming to external expectations.

I must remember that God created me with a distinct purpose and plan. By surrendering to His will and embracing who I truly am, I can live a life that is not only fulfilling but also inspiring to others.

My authenticity allows me to connect with others more deeply, foster genuine relationships, and positively impact the world. Embracing my authentic self is not just a personal journey but a spiritual one, guided by faith and trust in God's perfect plan for my life.

Transformation and New Beginnings

I am no longer the person I used to be; God has made something new from the old me. As a born-again believer, I have the incredible opportunity to experience a new beginning, a rebirth in Yeshua that transforms me into a new creation. My past no longer defines me; Yeshua's blood washed away the mistakes I made, the sins I committed, and the struggles I faced. I am free from the bondage of my past and can walk confidently in the new life that God has given me.

Freedom from the Past

One of the most powerful aspects of being born again is the realization that my past no longer holds power over me. The burdens of my previous life, the guilt and shame I carried, have been lifted. In Yeshua, I am a new creation, unbound by the limitations and failures of my former self. This transformation is not just a change in identity but a profound spiritual renewal that redefines who I am at my core.

Embracing the New Identity

Embracing this new identity requires me to let go of old ways of thinking and behaving. It means stepping into the fullness of the new me that God has created. I must consciously walk in the truth of who I am in Him, leaving behind the habits and patterns that no longer serve me. This transformation journey is ongoing, calling me to grow and evolve in my faith and character continuously.

Letting Go of the Past

It can be challenging to fully accept this new beginning, especially when past mistakes and regrets try to resurface. However, I must remember that holding onto these memories only hinders my progress. By acknowledging and learning from my past, I can release its hold on me and embrace the future with hope and optimism. Each day is an opportunity to start fresh, to create a new life filled with positivity and purpose.

With my rebirth in Yeshua comes a wealth of new possibilities. New friendships, opportunities, and ways of life await me as I step out in faith. Trusting in God's provision and plan, I can confidently pursue the path He has set before me. Embracing this new beginning means living with courage and optimism, knowing that the best is yet to come. My transformation is a testament to God's grace and the endless possibilities that lie ahead.

Overcoming Past Mistakes and Embracing Change

It can be easy to dwell on past mistakes and regrets, but holding onto them hinders my growth and progress. By acknowledging my past choices and learning from them, I can release the burden of guilt and shame that weighs me down.

Change is an inevitable part of life, and embracing it with an open heart and mind is essential for my personal development. Each new day offers a chance to start fresh, create a better life, and move forward with positivity and hope.

I have learned that my past does not define who I am today. The mistakes I made and the struggles I faced were part of my journey, but they did not determine my future.

By recognizing this, I can free myself from the chains of past regrets and open myself to new possibilities. Embracing change means letting go of the old and welcoming the new, trusting that each step I take is a step toward growth and improvement.

Trusting in my strength and resilience is crucial for overcoming challenges. Life is full of obstacles, but I can face them head-on by believing in my abilities.

I have the power to overcome any difficulties that come my way. I can navigate tough times with grace and determination by maintaining a positive mindset. This inner strength allows me to embrace change and see it as an opportunity for growth rather than a threat.

Learning from past mistakes is a vital part of personal growth. Instead of allowing these mistakes to define me, I use them as lessons to guide my future decisions.

By reflecting on what went wrong and understanding why it happened, I can make better choices moving forward. This process of self-reflection and learning is continuous, helping me to evolve, become wiser, and more resilient.

Each day is a new beginning, a chance to reinvent myself and pursue my dreams. I must embrace the opportunities that come my way and celebrate the progress I make.

By focusing on the present and the future rather than the past, I can create a life filled with positivity and hope. My past choices no longer define me; the person I am becoming truly matters. Embracing change with courage and optimism, I look forward to the endless possibilities.

Trusting in God's Plan

We are unique with our gifts, talents, and purpose. I have come to understand that God has a specific plan for my life that is tailor-made for my journey. Trusting in God's plan means having faith that He knows what is best for me, even when it doesn't align with my desires or expectations. Surrendering to His will allows me to find true fulfillment and purpose.

Seeing the Bigger Picture

There have been times when I struggled to see the bigger picture, moments when I questioned why certain things happened the way they did. However, prayer and reflection made me realize that God's plan is far greater than my limited perspective. His timing is perfect, and His ways are higher than mine. I can find peace and assurance in His plan by letting go of my need to control and understanding that He is guiding my steps.

Embracing New Opportunities

Trusting in God's plan also means being open to the new opportunities and paths He presents. Sometimes, I am called to step out of my comfort zone and venture into the unknown. These moments can be challenging but also opportunities for growth and transformation. I can face the future with confidence and hope by embracing the changes and trusting that God is leading me toward something more significant.

Finding Freedom in Trust

Trusting in God's plan gives me a profound sense of freedom. It allows me to let go of the anxieties and fears that often accompany uncertainty. Instead of worrying about the future, I can focus on living in the present and making the most of each day. Knowing that God is in control gives me the courage to pursue my dreams and live a life of purpose and meaning.

Trusting in God's plan means recognizing that I am not alone. God is always with me, guiding and supporting me every step of the way. His love and wisdom provide a foundation to build my life. By surrendering to His will and trusting in His plan, I can live a fulfilling life that aligns with His greater purpose.

Walking in Freedom and Abundance

As a believer, I am called to walk in abundance in every area of my life. This includes experiencing new blessings, such as opportunities, relationships, and financial provisions that God provides. Walking in freedom and abundance means trusting in God's provision and believing. He will bless me abundantly as I walk in obedience to His Word.

Embracing God's Provision

God's provision is not just about material wealth; it encompasses all aspects of life. I can experience peace, joy, love, and purpose by trusting in Him. This provision comes from deep faith and reliance on God's promises. I have learned to trust that God will meet my needs and provide for me in ways that go beyond my expectations.

Overcoming Strongholds

With my rebirth in Yeshua, I have the power to overcome the demons that once plagued me. Whether it be addiction, fear, insecurity, or any other stronghold, God has given me the authority to cast out these demons and walk in freedom. Confronting the darkness in my life and allowing God to bring healing and deliverance is a crucial part of my journey toward true freedom and abundance.

Living with Integrity and Purpose

Walking in freedom and abundance also means living a life of integrity and purpose. I am called to align my actions with God's Word and pursue His unique purpose for my life. This involves making choices that honor Him and reflect His love and grace. By living with integrity, I can experience the fullness of the abundant life that God has promised.

Celebrating New Beginnings

Each new day is a gift and an opportunity to embrace new beginnings. With my rebirth in Yeshua comes a wealth of new experiences and possibilities. Embracing these new beginnings with open arms and a hopeful heart allows me to walk confidently into the future God has prepared for me. It is a continuous growth and transformation journey filled with God's blessings and guidance.

Trusting in God's Promises

Ultimately, walking in freedom and abundance is about trusting God's promises and plans for my life. By surrendering to His will and believing in His goodness, I can live a life that is not only fulfilling but also abundant in every sense. God's love and grace are sufficient to cover my past, present, and future. Embracing this truth allows me to walk in the freedom and abundance He has destined for me.

Learning from Past Mistakes

Reflecting on my past mistakes allows me to gain valuable insights and wisdom that shape my journey forward. Instead of dwelling on regrets, I see these experiences as opportunities for growth and learning. Each mistake teaches me valuable lessons about myself, others, and the world around me. By acknowledging and understanding where I went wrong, I empower myself to make better choices in the future.

Through introspection and self-awareness, I uncover patterns and behaviors that may have led to past mistakes. This process of reflection enables me to identify areas for improvement and develop strategies to overcome similar challenges in the future. Rather than repeating the same errors, I use my past mistakes as stepping stones towards personal growth and development.

Learning from my past mistakes fosters humility and resilience within me. It reminds me that I am not perfect and that failure is a natural part of the human experience. Embracing this truth allows me to approach life with a sense of openness and curiosity, knowing that every setback is an opportunity for growth. I view my past mistakes not as failures but as valuable lessons that shape me into a stronger and more resilient individual.

Sharing my experiences of overcoming past mistakes can inspire and encourage others on their journeys. By being transparent about my struggles and the lessons I've learned, I create an atmosphere of authenticity and vulnerability. This fosters more profound connections with others facing similar challenges, offering them hope and guidance as they navigate their paths. In essence, learning from my past mistakes not only benefits me but also has the power to positively impact those around me.

Cultivating Inner Strength

Cultivating inner strength is a journey of self-discovery and resilience, where I intentionally nurture the qualities within me that empower me to face life's challenges with courage and grace. It involves developing a deep sense of self-awareness and tapping into my inherent resilience to navigate through adversity.

In times of difficulty, I draw upon my inner strength to persevere and overcome obstacles. This inner resilience is a guiding light, reminding me of my ability to weather storms and emerge stronger on the other side. Through mindfulness practices, prayer, and self-reflection, I continually strengthen this inner core, equipping myself to face whatever life may throw my way.

Cultivating inner strength involves embracing vulnerability and acknowledging my limitations. It is not about putting up walls or suppressing emotions but rather about having the courage to be authentic and vulnerable in adversity. By accepting myself fully, flaws and all, I cultivate a sense of inner resilience that allows me to easily navigate life's ups and downs.

Building inner strength empowers me to maintain a positive mindset even in challenges. It enables me to reframe obstacles as opportunities for growth and transformation rather than insurmountable barriers. This positive outlook fuels my determination and empowers me to persevere, no matter what challenges may come my way.

Cultivating inner strength is a lifelong journey that requires patience, self-love, and perseverance. It is about embracing my inherent resilience, tapping into my inner resources, and trusting my ability to navigate life's challenges with grace and courage. By continually nurturing this inner core, I empower myself to live a life of purpose, resilience, and fulfillment.

Seeking Divine Guidance

In the intricate tapestry of life, there are moments when I find myself at a crossroads, uncertain of which path to take or what decision to make. It is during these times of uncertainty that I turn to seek divine guidance, trusting in a higher power to illuminate my path and provide clarity amidst the fog of confusion. Seeking divine guidance is not merely a passive act but an intentional surrendering of my will to a greater wisdom beyond my understanding.

As I seek divine guidance, I first quiet my mind and open my heart to the whispers of the divine. Through prayer, meditation, and reflection, I create a sacred space to commune with the Holy and listen for gentle guidance. In this stillness, I find solace and peace, knowing that I am not alone but held in the loving embrace of a higher power who knows me intimately and cares for me deeply.

Divine guidance often comes unexpectedly – through a serendipitous encounter, a sudden insight, or a quiet inner knowing. It is not always loud or dramatic but subtle and gentle, like a whisper in the wind or a soft touch on the soul. I learned to discern these divine messages by tuning into my intuition and paying attention to the signs and synchronicities that unfold in my life.

Trusting in divine guidance requires surrendering my ego and letting go of the need to control outcomes. It involves relinquishing my attachment to a particular outcome and opening up to the greater possibilities that the divine has in store for me. In this surrender, I find liberation and freedom, knowing I am held in the loving embrace of a higher power guiding me toward my highest good.

Seeking divine guidance is not a one-time event but an ongoing practice that I cultivate daily. It is a way of living in alignment with divine will, trusting in the unfolding of life's divine plan with unwavering faith and devotion. In seeking divine guidance, I find clarity and direction, deepening my connection with the sacred and a profound sense of purpose and meaning in my life.

Embracing Personal Growth

Embracing personal growth is an intentional journey of self-discovery, transformation, and continuous improvement. It is a commitment I make to myself to strive for growth in all aspects of my life – mentally, emotionally, spiritually, and physically. This journey involves stepping out of my comfort zone, facing my fears, and embracing new opportunities for learning and development.

At the heart of embracing personal growth is a willingness to confront my limitations and challenge my existing beliefs and assumptions. I recognize that growth often requires discomfort and uncertainty, but through these challenges, I expand my horizons and unlock my full potential. With each step forward, I gain valuable insights and experiences that shape me into a more robust, wiser, and resilient individual.

Embracing personal growth involves cultivating a growth mindset – believing my abilities and intelligence can be developed through dedication and hard work. Instead of viewing setbacks as failures, I see them as opportunities for growth and learning. I approach challenges with optimism and resilience, knowing that each obstacle I overcome brings me one step closer to realizing my goals and aspirations.

As I journey toward personal growth, I am guided by a spirit of curiosity and exploration. I seek out new experiences, perspectives, and opportunities for self-discovery. Whether learning a new skill, pursuing a passion project, or engaging in meaningful conversations with others, I embrace every opportunity to expand my knowledge and broaden my horizons.

Embracing personal growth is a lifelong commitment to becoming the best version of myself. It is a journey of self-discovery, empowerment, and fulfillment that unfolds with each passing day. By embracing the challenges and opportunities that come my way, I embark on a transformative journey toward realizing my full potential and living a life of purpose and meaning.

Nurturing Meaningful Relationships

In the tapestry of life, relationships form the colorful threads that weave together the fabric of my existence. Nurturing meaningful relationships is not just a pursuit but a sacred duty—a commitment to fostering connections that enrich my life and the lives of those around me. It is about cultivating bonds built on trust, respect, and mutual understanding, where love flows freely and unconditionally.

At the heart of nurturing meaningful relationships lies the willingness to invest time, effort, and energy into building and maintaining connections with others. It requires me to be present and attentive, to listen with empathy and compassion, and to offer support and encouragement when needed. By prioritizing relationships in my life, I create a sense of belonging and community that nourishes my soul and brings joy and fulfillment to my days.

Nurturing meaningful relationships involves embracing vulnerability and authenticity in my interactions with others. It requires me to show up as my true self, flaws and all, and to allow others to do the same. I foster deeper connections based on trust and genuine intimacy by creating a safe space for openness and honesty. In sharing life's joys and struggles with others, I cultivate bonds that withstand the test of time and adversity.

Nurturing meaningful relationships is about celebrating the uniqueness and individuality of each person in my life. It involves honoring their perspectives, values, and experiences, even when they differ from mine. By embracing diversity and inclusivity, I create an environment where everyone feels seen, heard, and valued for who they are. In doing so, I cultivate a sense of unity and harmony that transcends boundaries and enriches the tapestry of my relationships.

Nurturing meaningful relationships is a journey of love, growth, and connection that unfolds one heartfelt interaction at a time. It is about sowing seeds of kindness and compassion, nurturing them with care and attention, and watching them blossom into beautiful expressions of love and friendship. By investing in meaningful relationships, I create a legacy of love that extends far beyond myself, enriching the lives of others and leaving a lasting impact on the world.

About the Author

A story of Rondell F Kinsey Jr from Syracuse, New York. A born again Christian who by the grace of God overcame many adversities. Rondell shares his experience, strength and hope on how finding faith in God brought him from an Ex-gang member, drug addicted sex addict, who was chasing a life-long dream of becoming a famous hip hop rapper to suffering from a cocaine addiction and hitting rock bottom and rebuilt his relationship with God becoming a solider in Christ's army and a vessel using his voice as a Christian content creator as well as an independent Christian recording artist to spread the Gospel of how the love of Jesus took him from once being lost and has now found his purpose thru Christ and Narcotics anonymous.

- The purpose of this book is to share my experience, strength and hope as well as paint a vivid picture on how God saved me from living a life of sin.

WHAT AM I UP TO NOW:

- Still reside in Syracuse, NY.
- Still clean and sober and apart of Narcotics anonymous program attending meetings regularly.

Founder of Chosen By Christ, LLC

- Owner of a small Christian apparel brand Called Chosen by Christ

Find on Instagram @chosenbychristclothing

- Christian Content Creator via social media and YouTube where he spreads the Gospel of Yeshua (Jesus Christ) and share his experience strength and hope to inspire and Uplift God's children.

Find on Instagram

@chosenbychrist_gospel

YouTube: Gerald Kinsey Jr

@geraldkinseyjr

Writing and Recording Music:

You can find his new single "Hurt the ones I love" under his stage name Gerald Kinsey available on all platforms.

Find on IG @therealgeraldkinsey